Statutes of Limitation in Federal Criminal Cases: An Overview

Charles Doyle
Senior Specialist in American Public Law

October 1, 2012

Congressional Research Service
7-5700
www.crs.gov
RL31253

CRS Report for Congress
Prepared for Members and Committees of Congress

Summary

A statute of limitations dictates the time period within which a legal proceeding must begin. The purpose of a statute of limitations in a criminal case is to ensure the prompt prosecution of criminal charges and thereby spare the accused of the burden of having to defend against stale charges after memories may have faded or evidence is lost.

There is no statute of limitations for federal crimes punishable by death, nor for certain federal crimes of terrorism, nor, since passage of the Adam Walsh Child Protection and Safety Act (2006) (P.L. 109-248), for certain federal sex offenses. Prosecution for most other federal crimes must begin within five years of the commitment of the offense. There are exceptions. Some types of crimes are subject to a longer period of limitation; some circumstances suspend or extend the otherwise applicable period of limitation.

Arson, art theft, certain crimes against financial institutions and various immigration offenses all carry statutes of limitation longer than the five year standard. Regardless of the applicable statute of limitations, the period may be extended or the running of the period suspended or tolled under a number of circumstances such as when the accused is a fugitive or when the case involves charges of child abuse, bankruptcy, wartime fraud against the government, or DNA evidence.

Ordinarily, the statute of limitations begins to run as soon as the crime has been completed. Although the federal crime of conspiracy is complete when one of the plotters commits an affirmative act in its name, the period for conspiracies begins with the last affirmative act committed in furtherance of the scheme. Other so-called continuing offenses include various possession crimes and some that impose continuing obligations to register or report.

Limitation-related constitutional challenges arise most often under the Constitution's ex post facto and due process clauses. The federal courts have long held that a statute of limitations may be enlarged retroactively as long as the previously applicable period of limitation has not expired. The Supreme Court recently confirmed that view; the ex post facto proscription precludes legislative revival of an expired period of limitation. Due process condemns pre-indictment delays even when permitted by the statute of limitations if the prosecution wrongfully caused the delay and the accused's defense suffered actual, substantial harm as a consequence.

A list of federal statutes of limitation in criminal cases and a rough chart of comparable state provisions are attached. This report is available in an abbreviated form as CRS Report RS21121, *Statutes of Limitation in Federal Criminal Cases: A Sketch*, without the attachments, footnotes, or attributions to authority found here.

Contents

Introduction 1
Prosecution at Any Time 2
Limits by Crime 3
Suspension and Extension 3
    Child Protection 4
    DNA 4
    Concealing Bankruptcy Assets 5
    Wartime Statute of Limitations 5
    Indictment or Information 6
    Foreign Evidence 7
    Fugitives 10
Conspiracies and Continuing Offenses 11
    Constitutional Considerations 14

Appendixes

Appendix A. Periods of Limitation for Specific Federal Crimes 18
Appendix B. State Felony Statutes of Limitation 30

Contacts

Author Contact Information 35

Introduction

The Constitution's speedy trial clause[1] protects the criminally accused against unreasonable delays between his indictment and trial. Before indictment, the statutes of limitation, and in extreme circumstances, the due process clauses [2] protect the accused from unreasonable delays. The anti-terrorism measures of the USA PATRIOT Act [3] made substantial alterations in the statutes of limitation that govern a number of federal crimes. This is an overview of federal law relating to the statutes of limitation in criminal cases, including those changes produced by the act.

The phrase "statute of limitations" refers to the time period within which formal criminal charges must be brought after a crime has been committed.[4] "The purpose of a statute of limitations is to limit exposure to criminal prosecution to a certain fixed period of time following the occurrence of those acts the legislature has decided to punish by criminal sanctions. Such a limitation is designed to protect individuals from having to defend themselves against charges when the basic facts may have become obscured by the passage of time and to minimize the danger of official punishment because of acts in the far-distant past. Such a time limit may also have the salutary effect of encouraging law enforcement officials promptly to investigate suspected criminal activity." [5] Therefore, in most instances, prosecutions are barred if the defendant points out that there was no indictment or other formal charge within the time period dictated by the statute of limitations.[6]

Statutes of limitation are creatures of statute. The common law recognized no period of limitation.[7] An indictment could be brought at any time. Limitations are recognized today only to the extent that a statute or due process dictates their recognition.[8] Congress and most state legislatures have enacted statutes of limitation, but declare that prosecution for some crimes may be brought at any time.[9]

---

[1] U.S. Const. Amend. VI.

[2] U.S. Const. Amends. V and XIV.

[3] P.L. 107-56, 115 Stat. 809 (2001).

[4] BLACK'S LAW DICTIONARY 1546 (9th ed. 2009).

[5] *Toussie v. United States*, 397 U.S. 112, 114-15 (1970).

[6] The statute of limitations is an affirmative defense that can be waived either explicitly, by pleading guilty, or by failure to raise it at or before trial, *United States v. Wilbur*, 674 F.3d 1160, 1177 (9th Cir. 2012) (affirmative defense, waived if not raised); *United States v. Hsu*, 669 F.3d 112, 117-18 (2d Cir. 2012)(waiver by guilty plea); *United States v. Flood*, 635 F.3d 1255, 1258 (10th Cir. 2011)(express waiver); *United States v. Baldwin*, 414 F.3d 791, 795 (7th Cir. 2005)(affirmative defense); *United States v. Titterington*, 374 F.3d 453, 458 (6th Cir. 2004)(affirmative defense); *United States v. Jake*, 281 F.3d 123, 129 (3d Cir. 2002)(waived by failure to raise at or before trial); *United States v. Mulderig*, 120 F.3d 534, 540 (5th Cir. 1997)(same); *United States v. Specter*, 55 F.3d 22, 24 (1st Cir. 1995)(waivable, affirmative defense); *United States v. Wilson*, 26 F.3d 142, 155 (D.C. 1994)(waivable).

[7] *Doggett v. United States*, 505 U.S. 647, 667 (1992)(Thomas, J., dissenting), citing inter alia, 2 STEPHEN, A HISTORY OF THE CRIMINAL LAW OF ENGLAND 1, 2 (1883).

[8] At some point events pass into history and due process restricts the extent to which they may be resurrected to build a criminal accusation, with or without an applicable statute of limitations, *United States v. Marion*, 404 U.S. 307, 324 (1971).

[9] Capsulized descriptions of the various state criminal statutes of limitation governing felony prosecutions are appended.

Federal statutes of limitation are as old as federal crimes. When the Founders assembled in the First Congress, they passed not only the first federal criminal laws but made prosecution under those laws subject to specific statutes of limitation.[10] Similar provisions continue to this day. Federal capital offenses may be prosecuted at any time,[11] but unless some more specific arrangement has been made a general five year statute of limitations covers all other federal crimes.[12] Some of the exceptions to the general rule, like those of the USA PATRIOT Act, identify longer periods for particular crimes.[13] Others suspend or extend the applicable period under certain circumstances such as the flight of the accused,[14] or during time of war.[15]

Prosecution at Any Time

Aside from capital offenses,[16] crimes which Congress associated with terrorism may be prosecuted at any time if they result in a death or serious injury or create a foreseeable risk of death or serious injury.[17] Although the crimes were selected because they are often implicated in acts of terrorism, a terrorist defendant is not a prerequisite to an unlimited period for prosecution.[18] A third category of crimes that may be prosecuted at any time consists of various designated federal child abduction and sex offenses.[19]

---

[10] Except for murder and forgery, the statute of limitations for the prosecution of all federal capital offenses is three years; the statute of limitations for all noncapital crimes is two years, 1 Stat. 119 (1790).

[11] 18 U.S.C. 3281.

[12] "Except as otherwise expressly provided by law, no person shall be prosecuted, tried, or punished for any offense, not capital, unless the indictment is found or information is instituted within five years next after such offense shall have been committed," 18 U.S.C. 3282.

[13] 18 U.S.C. 3286.

[14] 18 U.S.C. 3290.

[15] 18 U.S.C. 3287.

[16] "An indictment for any offense punishable by death may be found at any time without limitation," 18 U.S.C. 3281. Between the Supreme Court's decision in *Furman v. Georgia*, 408 U.S. 238 (1972), and passage of the Violent Crime Control and Law Enforcement Act of 1994, 108 Stat. 1796, the death penalty authorized by federal capital offense statutes could not be constitutionally imposed. The question arose whether the term "offenses punishable by death" in the statute of limitations referred to offenses made capital by statute or only to offenses for which the death penalty might constitutionally be imposed. The courts concluded that Congress intended the term to refer to offenses which it made capital by statute. *United States v. Emery*, 186 F.3d 921, 924 (8th Cir. 1999); *United States v. Edwards*, 159 F.3d 1117, 1128 (8th Cir. 1998); *United States v. Manning*, 56 F.3d 1188, 1196 (9th Cir. 1995). A list of the federal capital offenses is appended. The list includes those crimes made capital by operation of other provisions of law such as 18 U.S.C. 3559(f)(murder of a child during the course a federal crime of violence) and 18 U.S.C. 2245 (murder committed during the course of designated federal sex offenses).

[17] 18 U.S.C. 3286(b)("Notwithstanding any other law, an indictment may be found or an information instituted at any time without limitation for any offense listed in Section 2332b(g)(5)(B), if the commission of such offense resulted in, or created a foreseeable risk of, death or serious bodily injury to another person"). A list of crimes cross referenced in 18 U.S.C.2332b(g)(5)(B) is appended.

[18] 18 U.S.C. 2332b(g)(5) defines a federal crime of terrorism as "an offense that – (A) is calculated to influence or affect the conduct of a government by intimidation or coercion, or to retaliate against government conduct; and (B) is a violation of" one of list of terrorism-associated offenses. The list of crimes which Section 3286(b) makes prosecutable at any time consists of those crimes listed in 18 U.S.C. 2332b(g)(5)(*B*)(emphasis added). Had Congress wished the waiver of the statutes of limitation to apply only to terrorists accused of these offenses presumably it would have referred to 18 U.S.C. 2332b(g)(5), i.e., both 2332b(g)(5)(A) and (B), rather than simply to 18 U.S.C. 2332b(g)(5)(B) as it did.

[19] 18 U.S.C. 3299 ("Notwithstanding any other law, an indictment may be found or an information instituted at any time without limitation for any offense under Section 1201 [kidnaping] involving a minor victim, and for any felony (continued...)

Limits by Crime

Although the majority of federal crimes are governed by the general five year statute of limitations, Congress has chosen longer periods for specific types of crimes – 20 years for the theft of art work;[20] 10 years for arson,[21] for certain crimes against financial institutions,[22] and for immigration offenses;[23] and eight years for the nonviolent violations of the terrorism-associated statutes which may be prosecuted at any time if committed under violent circumstances.[24] Investigative difficulties[25] or the seriousness of the crime[26] seem to have provided the rationale for enlargement of the time limit for prosecuting these offenses beyond the five year standard.

Suspension and Extension

The five year rule may yield to circumstances other than the type of crime to be prosecuted. For example, an otherwise applicable limitation period may be suspended or extended in cases

---

(...continued)
under Chapter 109A, 110 (except for Section 2257 and 2257A), or 117, or Section 1591 [sex trafficking of an adult by force or fraud or of a child]").

The felonies in Chapters 109A, 110 and 117 include violations of 18 U.S.C. 2241 (aggravated sexual abuse), 2242 (sexual abuse), 2243 (sexual abuse of a ward or child), 2244 (abusive sexual contact), 2245 (sexual abuse resulting in death), 2250 (failure to register as a sex offender), 2251 (sexual exploitation of children), 2251A (selling or buying children), 2252 (transporting, distributing or selling child sexually exploitive material), 2252A (transporting or distributing child pornography), 2252B (misleading names on the Internet), 2260 (making child sexually exploitative material overseas for export to the U.S.), 2421 (transportation for illicit sexual purposes), 2422 (coercing or enticing travel for illicit sexual purposes), 2423 (travel involving illicit sexual activity with a child), 2424 (filing false immigration statement), 2425 (interstate transmission of information about a child relating to illicit sexual activity).

[20] "No person shall be prosecuted, tried, or punished for a violation of or conspiracy to violate Section 668 unless the indictment is returned or the information is filed within 20 years after the commission of the offense," 18 U.S.C. 3294.

[21] "No person shall be prosecuted, tried, or punished for any non-capital offense under Section 81 [arson in the special maritime or territorial jurisdiction of the United States] or subsection (f), (h), or (i) of Section 844 [use of fire or explosives to commit a federal offense, and burning or bombing of federal property or property used in or in activities affecting interstate or foreign commerce] unless the indictment is found or the information is instituted not later than 10 years after the date on which the offense was committed," 18 U.S.C. 3295.

[22] "No person shall be prosecuted, tried, or punished for a violation of, or a conspiracy to violate – (1) Section 215, 656, 657, 1005, 1006, 1007, 1014, 1033, or 1344; (2) Section 1341 or 1343 [mail and wire fraud], if the offense affects a financial institution; or (3) Section 1963 [(RICO) racketeer influenced and corrupt organizations], to the extent that the racketeering activity involves a violation of Section 1344 [bank fraud] – unless the indictment is returned or the information is filed within 10 years after the commission of the offense," 18 U.S.C. 3293.

[23] "No person shall be prosecuted, tried, or punished for violation of any provision of Sections 1423 to 1428, inclusive, of Chapter 69 [nationality and citizenship offenses] and Sections 1541 to 1544, inclusive, of Chapter 75 [passport and visa offenses] of Title 18 of the United States Code, or for conspiracy to violate any of such Sections, unless the indictment is found or the information is instituted within 10 years after the commission of the offense," 18 U.S.C. 3291.

[24] "Notwithstanding Section 3282, no person shall be prosecuted, tried, or punished for any noncapital offense involving a violation of any provision listed in Section 2332b(g)(5)(B) [terrorist offenses], or a violation 112, 351(e), 1361, or 1751(e) of this title, or Section 46504, 46505, or 46506 of Title 49, unless the indictment is found or the information is instituted within eight years after the offense was committed...." 18 U.S.C. 3286(a).

[25] *See e.g.*, H.Rept. 82-167, at 2-3 (1951); H.Rept. 98-907, at 2 (1984), *reprinted in*, 1984 U.S.C.C.A.N. 3578, 3578-579.

[26] *Administration's Draft Anti-Terrorism Act of 2001: Hearings Before the House Comm. on the Judiciary*, 107th Cong., 1st Sess. at 60 (2001).

involving child abuse,[27] the concealment of the assets of an estate in bankruptcy,[28] wartime fraud against the government,[29] dismissal of original charges,[30] fugitives,[31] foreign evidence,[32] or DNA evidence.[33]

Child Protection

The child protection section, 18 U.S.C. 3283, permits an indictment or information charging kidnaping, or sexual abuse, or physical abuse, of a child under the age of 18 to be filed within the longer of 10 years or the life of the victim.[34] Section 3299 (enacted in 2006),[35] which eliminates the statute of limitations in cases of child abduction and sex offenses against children, supersedes §3283 wherever the two overlap.

DNA

There are two DNA provisions. One, 18 U.S.C. 3297, suspends any applicable statute of limitations for the time required to identify an individual when DNA evidence implicates his involvement in a felony offense.[36] The other, 18 U.S.C. 3282(b), suspends the statute of limitations for federal sexual abuse violations by means of an indictment using a DNA profile alone to identify the person charged.[37] Neither provision comes into play when the offense involves sexual abuse of a child or child abduction. As noted earlier, prosecution for such crimes may be brought at any time under 18 U.S.C. 3299.

Section 3282(b) is the narrower of the two DNA provisions. It only applies to offenses proscribed in 18 U.S.C. ch. 109A. Chapter 109A outlaws abusive sexual contact, sexual abuse, and aggravated sexual abuse when any of these offenses is committed in a federal prison, or within

---

[27] 18 U.S.C. 3283.

[28] 18 U.S.C. 3284.

[29] 18 U.S.C. 3287.

[30] 18 U.S.C. 3288, 3289.

[31] 18 U.S.C. 3290.

[32] 18 U.S.C. 3292.

[33] 18 U.S.C. 3282(b), 3297.

[34] "No statute of limitations that would otherwise preclude prosecution for an offense involving the sexual or physical abuse, or kidnaping, of a child under the age of 18 years shall preclude such prosecution during the life of the child, or for 10 years after the offense, whichever is longer," 18 U.S.C. 3283.

[35] See text at note 16, supra.

[36] 18 U.S.C . 3297 ("In a case in which DNA testing implicates an identified person in the commission of a felony, no statute of limitations that would otherwise preclude prosecution of the offense shall preclude such prosecution until a period of time following the implication of the person by DNA testing has elapsed that is equal to the otherwise applicable limitation period").

[37] 18 U.S.C. 3282(b)("(1) In general. - In any indictment for an offense under chapter 109A for which the identity of the accused is unknown, it shall be sufficient to describe the accused as an individual whose name is unknown, but who has a particular DNA profile. (2) Exception. - Any indictment described under paragraph (1), which is found not later than 5 years after the offense under chapter 109A is committed, shall not be subject to - (A) the limitations period described under subsection (a); and (B) the provisions of chapter 208 until the individual is arrested or served with a summons in connection with the charges contained in the indictment. (3) Defined term. - For purposes of this subsection, the term 'DNA profile' means a set of DNA identification characteristics").

the special maritime or territorial jurisdiction of the United States.[38] Section 3282(b) also suspends the provisions of the Speedy Trial Act that would otherwise come to life with the filing of an indictment in such cases.[39] Section 3282(b), however, reaches only those cases in which the statute of limitations has not already expired.[40]

Section 3297 applies to any federal felony. Rather than suspend the statute of limitations, it marks the beginning of the period of limitation, not from the commission of the crime, but from the time when DNA testing implicates an individual.

Concealing Bankruptcy Assets

The statute of limitations on offenses which involve concealing bankruptcy assets does not begin to run until a final decision discharging or refusing to discharge the debtor: "The concealment of assets of a debtor in a case under Title 11 shall be deemed to be a continuing offense until the debtor shall have been finally discharged or a discharge denied, and the period of limitations shall not begin to run until such final discharge or denial of discharge," 18 U.S.C. 3284. When a discharge determination is impossible because of the dismissal of bankruptcy proceedings or want of a timely discharge petition or for any other reason, the statute of limitations runs from the date of the event when discharge becomes impossible.[41]

Wartime Statute of Limitations

Section 3287 establishes a suspension of the statute of limitations covering wartime frauds committed against the United States [42] that allows for prosecution at any time up to five years after the end of the war.[43] At one time, it could be said with some conviction that §3287 "appears

---

[38] 18 U.S.C. 2244, 2242, and 2241, respectively. Chapter 109A also criminalizes sexual abuse of a ward and aggravated sexual abuse of a child, but again those offenses may be prosecuted at any time by operation of 18 U.S.C. 3299.

[39] 18 U.S.C. 3282(b)(2)(B); 18 U.S.C. 3161-3174 (Speedy Trial Act).

[40] 18 U.S.C. 3282(b)(2)(A). The Constitution prohibits revival of an expired statute of limitations, *Stogner v. California*, 539 U.S. 607 (2003).

[41] *United States v. Gilbert*, 136 F.3d 1451, 1454-455 (11th Cir. 1998); *United States v. Dolan*, 120 F.3d 856, 867-68 (8th Cir. 1997), both citing, *United States v. Guglielmini*, 425 F.2d 439 (2d Cir. 1970); and *Rudin v. United States*, 254 F.2d 45 (6th Cir. 1958).

[42] "When the United States is at war or Congress has enacted a specific authorization for the use of the Armed Forces, as described in section 5(b) of the War Powers Resolution (50 U.S.C. 1544(b)), the running of any statute of limitations applicable to any offense (1) involving fraud or attempted fraud against the United States or any agency thereof in any manner, whether by conspiracy or not, or (2) committed in connection with the acquisition, care, handling, custody, control or disposition of any real or personal property of the United States, or (3) committed in connection with the negotiation, procurement, award, performance, payment for, interim financing, cancelation, or other termination or settlement, of any contract, subcontract, or purchase order which is connected with or related to the prosecution of the war or directly connected with or related to the authorized use of the Armed Forces, or with any disposition of termination inventory by any war contractor or Government agency, shall be suspended until 5 years after the termination of hostilities as proclaimed by a Presidential proclamation, with notice to Congress, or by a concurrent resolution of Congress. Definitions of terms in section 103 of title 41 shall apply to similar terms used in this section. For purposes of applying such definitions in this section, the term 'war' includes a specific authorization for the use of the Armed Forces, as described in section 5(b) of the War Powers Resolution (50 U.S.C. 1544(b))," 18 U.S.C. 3287.

[43] "Although the language of [18 U.S.C. 3287] would seem to allow the Government to indict any frauds against the United States that occurred up to the end of the suspension period plus the relevant statute of limitations, the Supreme Court in *United States v. Smith*, 342 U.S. 225 (1952), held that §3287 only applied to crimes committed after the (continued...)

to have only been used in cases that involved conduct during or shortly after World War II" and none since.[44] That is no longer the case.[45]

In 2008, Congress amended the section to make it clear that the provision covers misconduct during both declared wars and periods of armed conflict for which Congress has explicitly authorized use of the Armed Forces.[46] The same amendment extended the period of suspension from three to five years.[47] The provision applies to crimes related to conduct of the conflict as well as those that are not.[48] The offense, however, must "involve the defrauding of the United States in [some] pecuniary manner or in a manner concerning property."[49] The provision's five year clock begins to run with the end of the war or conflict, but there is some difference of opinion over whether a formal termination must come first.[50]

Indictment or Information

The statute of limitations runs until an indictment or information is returned.[51] There is, however, some question about the impact of sealing the indictment upon its return. The Federal Rules of Criminal Procedure allow the magistrate to whom the indictment is returned to seal it until the defendant is apprehended or released on bail.[52] Some of the courts seem troubled when they believe that the seal has been applied for purposes of tactical advantage rather than to prevent the escape of the accused.[53]

If the indictment or information is subsequently dismissed, federal law gives the government an additional six months (30 days if the indictment or information is dismissed on appeal and there is

---

(...continued)
triggering of the suspension of limitation but before the termination of hostilities. *Id.* at 228," *United States v. Pfluger*, 685 F.3d 481, 484 (5th Cir. 2012)(parallel Supreme Court citations omitted).

[44] *United States v. Shelton*, 816 F.Supp. 1132, 1134-135 (W.D.Tex. 1993).

[45] See e.g., *United States v. Pfluger*, 685 F.3d at 484 n.5, and the cases cited therein.

[46] P.L. 110-329, §8117, 122 Stat. 3647 (2008), 18 U.S.C. 3287.

[47] *Id.*

[48] *United States v. Prosperi*, 573 F.Supp.2d 436, 441-42 (D.Mass. 2008), citing inter alia, *United States v. Grainger*, 346 U.S. 235 (1953).

[49] *Bridges v. United States*, 346 U.S. 209, 220 (1953).

[50] *United States v. Pfluger*, 685 F.3d at 443-64 (holding that formal termination is required and noting a conflicting view in *United States v. Prosperi*, 573 F.Supp.2d at 454-55).

[51] *United States v. McMillian*, 600 F.3d 434, 444 (5th Cir. 2010)("Once an indictment is filed, the limitations period is tolled on the charges set forth in the indictment"); *United States v. Hickey*, 580 F.3d 922, 929 (9th Cir. 2009); *United States v. Milstein*, 401 F.3d 53, 67 (2d Cir. 2005); *United States v. Garcia*, 268 F.3d 407, 411 (6th Cir. 2001).

[52] F.R.Crim.P. 6(e)(4).

[53] *United States v. Ellis*, 622 F.3d 784, 792 (7th Cir. 2010)("The circuits are divided on whether the sealing of an indictment affects when the indictment is 'found' for purposes of the statute of limitations. The Tenth Circuit has held that an indictment is 'found' under §3284(a) whenever it is returned by the grand jury; sealing the indictment has no effect on this date. *United States v. Thompson*, 287 F.3d 1244, 1248-252 (10th Cir. 2002). But other circuits have held that sealing matters, at least in one sense; these circuits have held that an indictment is not 'found' for purposes of §3284(a) if it was *improperly* sealed and the improper sealing prejudiced to the defendant. *See, e.g. United States v. Bracy*, 67 F.3d1421, 1426 (9th Cir. 1995); *United States v. Sharpe*, 995 F.2d 49, 51-52 (5th Cir. 1993)(per curiam); *United States v. Muse*, 633 F.3d 1041, 1043-44 (2d Cir. 1980)(en banc)"); see also, *United States v. Richard*, 943 F.2d 115, 118-19 (1st Cir. 1991); *United States v. Larkin*, 875 F.2d 168, 170-72 (8th Cir. 1989); *United States v. Wright*, 343 F.3d 849, 857 (6th Cir. 2003); Stinson, *Secret Indictments: How to Discourage Them, How to Make Them Fair*, 2 DREXEL LAW REVIEW 104, 145 (2009)(arguing that "[c]urrent sealing practice raises serious due process concerns").

a grand jury with jurisdiction in place).⁵⁴ Beyond the extension here, when a timely indictment is dismissed pursuant to a plea agreement under which the defendant pleads to other charges, the statute of limitations ordinarily begins again for the dismissed charges unless the defendant has waived as part of the plea agreement.⁵⁵ The statute of limitations remains tolled if the original indictment is replaced by a superseding indictment, as long as the superseding indictment does not substantially alter the original charge.⁵⁶

Foreign Evidence

Section 3292 was enacted to compensate for the delays the Justice Department experienced when it sought to secure bank records and other evidence located overseas.⁵⁷ It provides that:

---

⁵⁴ "Whenever an indictment or information charging a felony is dismissed for any reason after the period prescribed by the applicable statute of limitations has expired, a new indictment may be returned in the appropriate jurisdiction within six calendar months of the date of the dismissal of the indictment or information, or, in the event of an appeal, within 60 days of the date the dismissal of the indictment or information becomes final, or, if no regular grand jury is in session in the appropriate jurisdiction when the indictment or information is dismissed, within six calendar months of the date when the next regular grand jury is convened, which new indictment shall not be barred by any statute of limitations. This section does not permit the filing of a new indictment or information where the reason for the dismissal was the failure to file the indictment or information within the period prescribed by the applicable statute of limitations, or some other reason that would bar a new prosecution," 18 U.S.C. 3288.

"Whenever an indictment or information charging a felony is dismissed for any reason before the period prescribed by the applicable statute of limitations has expired, and such period will expire within six calendar months of the date of the dismissal of the indictment or information, a new indictment may be returned in the appropriate jurisdiction within six calendar months of the expiration of the applicable statute of limitations, or, in the event of an appeal, within 60 days of the date the dismissal of the indictment or information becomes final or, if no regular grand jury is in session in the appropriate jurisdiction at the expiration of the applicable statute of limitations, within six calendar months of the date when the next regular grand jury is convened, which new indictment shall not be barred by any statute of limitations. This section does not permit the filing of a new indictment or information where the reason for the dismissal was the failure to file the indictment or information within the period prescribed by the applicable statute of limitations, or some other reason that would bar a new prosecution," 18 U.S.C. 3289.

⁵⁵ *United States v. Gilchrist*, 215 F.3d 333, 238-39 (3d Cir. 2000); *United States v. Midgley*, 142 F.3d 174, 177-79 (3d Cir. 1998); *United States v. Podde*, 105 F.3d 813, 818-20 (2d Cir. 1997). 18 U.S.C. 3296(a)("Notwithstanding any other provision of this chapter, any counts of an indictment or information that are dismissed pursuant to a plea agreement shall be reinstated by the District Court if - (1) the counts sought to be reinstated were originally filed within the applicable limitations period; (2) the counts were dismissed pursuant to a plea agreement approved by the District Court under which the defendant pled guilty to other charges; (3) the guilty plea was subsequently vacated on the motion of the defendant; and (4) the United States moves to reinstate the dismissed counts within 60 days of the date on which the order vacating the plea becomes final").

⁵⁶ *United States v. Yielding*, 657 F.3d 688, 703-704 (8th Cir. 2011)("For limitations purposes, a superseding indictment filed while the original indictment is validly pending relates back to the time of filing of the original indictment if it does not substantially broaden or amend the original charges.... To determine whether a superseding indictment substantially broadens or amends a pending timely indictment, we agree with other courts that it is appropriate to consider whether the additional pleadings allege violations of a different statute, contain different elements, rely on different evidence, or expose the defendant to a potentially greater sentence. The touchstone of this analysis is whether the original indictment provided the defendant with fair notice of the subsequent charges against him. *United States v. McMilian*, 600 F.3d 434, 444 (5th Cir. 2010); *United States v. Munoz-Franco*, 487 F.3d 25, 53 (1st Cir. 2007); *United States v. Salmonese*, 353 [F.3d. 608, 622 (2d Cir. 2003)]; *United States v. Smith*, 197 F.3d 225, 229 (6th Cir. 1999); *see also, United States v. Qayyum*, 451 F.3d 1214, 1218 (10th Cir. 2006); *United States v. Daniels*, 387 F.3d 636, 642 (7th Cir. 2004); *United States v. Ratcliff*, 245 F.3d 1246, 1253 (11th Cir. 2001); *United States v. Oliva*, 46 F.3d 320, 324 (3d Cir. 1995); *United States v. Snowden*, 770 F.2d 393, 398 (4th Cir. 1985).

⁵⁷ H.Rept 98-907, at 2-3 (1984), *reprinted in* 1984 U.S.C.C.A.N. 3578, 3578-579; *Foreign Evidence Rules Amendment: Hearing Before the Subcomm. on Criminal Justice of the House Comm. on the Judiciary*, 98th Cong., 2d Sess. 15 (1984)(testimony of Dep.Ass't Att'y Gen. Mark Richard).

> (a)(1) Upon application of the United States, filed before return of an indictment, indicating that evidence of an offense is in a foreign country, the district court before which a grand jury is impaneled to investigate the offense shall suspend the running of the statute of limitations for the offense if the court finds by a preponderance of the evidence that an official request has been made for such evidence and that it reasonably appears, or reasonably appeared at the time the request was made, that such evidence is, or was, in such foreign country.
>
> (2) The court shall rule upon such application not later than thirty days after the filing of the application.
>
> (b) Except as provided in subsection (c) of this section, a period of suspension under this section shall begin on the date on which the official request is made and end on the date on which the foreign court or authority takes final action on the request.
>
> (c) The total of all periods of suspension under this section with respect to an offense – (1) shall not exceed three years; and (2) shall not extend a period within which a criminal case must be initiated for more than six months if all foreign authorities take final action before such period would expire without regard to this section.
>
> (d) As used in this section, the term "official request" means a letter rogatory, a request under a treaty or convention, or any other request for evidence made by a court of the United States or an authority of the United States having criminal law enforcement responsibility, to a court or other authority of a foreign country.

Construction of Section 3292 has been something less than uniform, thus far.[58] The courts are divided over whether the target of the grand jury or the subject of the foreign evidence sought may contest the government's application when it is filed or whether the application may be filed ex parte with an opportunity for the accused to contest suspension following indictment.[59] By the same token, it is less certain whether the phrase indicating that the application must be filed with "the district court before which a grand jury is impaneled to investigate the offense," means that the application must relate to a specific grand jury investigation or may be filed in anticipation of such an investigation.[60] On the related issue of when an application may be filed, one court has ruled that the government may seek the suspension either to allow it to obtain foreign evidence or

---

[58] Abramovsky & Edelstein, *Time for Final Action on 18 U.S.C. 3292*, 21 MICHIGAN JOURNAL OF INTERNATIONAL LAW 941 (2000).

[59] Compare, *In re Grand Jury Investigation*, 3 F.Supp. 2d 82, 83 (D.Mass. 1998)("Nothing in section 3292, however, expressly contemplates secretly extending certain statutes of limitation as to certain individuals.... Moreover, this Court general eschews ex parte practice whenever possible, since action ex parte so fundamentally undercuts the values secured by the adversary process), with, *United States v. Little*, 667 F.3d 220, 225 (2d Cir. 2012)("Nowhere in §3292 does it state that the party whose statute of limitation is being suspended is entitled to notice or a hearing"); *United States v. Hoffecker*, 530 F.3d 137, 168 (3d Cir. 2008); *United States v. Torres*, 318 F.3d 1058, 1061 (11th Cir. 2003) *United States v. Wilson*, 249 F.3d 366, 371 (5th Cir. 2001); *DeGeroge v. U.S. District Court*, 219 F.3d 930, 937 (9th Cir. 2000).

[60] Compare, *United States v. O'Neill*, 952 F.Supp. 831, 833 (D.D.C. 1996)("The government can only request that statutes of limitation be tolled for offenses under investigation by the grand jury"), with, *DeGeorge v. U.S. District Court*, 219 F.3d at 939-40 (denial of mandamus)(characterizing the statement in *O'Neill* as dicta and declining to find clear error in a contrary lower court decision), *on appeal*, 380 F.3d 1203, 1214; but see, *United States v. Meador*, 138 F.3d 986, 994 (5th Cir. 1998) ("The purpose of §3292, apparent from its structure and legislative history, is to compensate for delays attendant in obtaining records from other countries. This provision should not be an affirmative benefit to prosecutors, suspending the limitations period, pending completion of an investigation, whenever evidence is located in a foreign land. It is not a statutory grant of authority to extend the limitations period by three years at the prosecutors' option").

to compensate it for time expended to acquire the evidence prior to the application.[61] Another has held that the extension cannot be had when the evidence sought by the government is in its possession at the time of the application.[62] Still others cannot agree on whether the request may revive an expired statute of limitations.[63]

The statute demands that the government bear the burden of establishing to the court its right to a suspension by a preponderance of the evidence.[64] The Second Circuit has pointed out, however, that the statute sets out two slightly different preponderance standards, a simple preponderance standard for the fact a request has been made, and slightly less demanding one (preponderance that it "reasonably appears") for the fact that the evidence sought exists overseas.[65] The government must do more than present unsworn, conclusionary statements to meet its burden,[66] but "something of evidentiary value" on point will ordinarily do.[67]

As for the nature of the overseas evidence, it is no bar to suspension that the evidence might be obtained in this country or that without it the grand jury has enough evidence to indict.[68] On the other hand, the court may not suspend, if the government has already received the foreign evidence at the time when it submits its application for suspension.[69]

The suspension begins when the government submits its official request to a foreign source.[70] It ends when the foreign entity takes "final action" on the request.[71] When that occurs may be a matter of some dispute. Some courts suggest that final action occurs with a dispositive response,

---

[61] *United States v. Miller*, 830 F.2d 1073, 1076 (9th Cir. 1987).

[62] *United States v. Atiyeh*, 402 F.3d 354, 362-67 (3d Cir. 2005).

[63] Compare, *United States v. Kozeny*, 541 F.3d 166, (2d Cir. 2008), and *United States v. Brody*, 621 F.Supp.2d 1196, 1999-1201 (D.Utah 2009), with, *United States v. Bischel*, 61 F.3d 1429 (9th Cir. 1995), and *United States v. Hoffecker*, 530 F.3d 137, 164 n.4 (3d Cir. 2008).

[64] 18 U.S.C. 3292(a)(1); *United States v. Wilson*, 249 F.3d at 373; *United States v. Trainor*, 376 F.3d 1325, 1330 (11th Cir. 2004).

[65] *United States v. Little*, 667 F.3d 220, 225 (2d Cir. 2012)("The statute therefore requires a district court to suspend the running of a statute of limitations upon an appropriate application showing: (1) that evidence of an offense being investigated by a grand jury is in a foreign country; and (2) that such evidence has been officially requested. According to the statute, the preponderance-of-the-evidence standard applies when determining whether the United States has made an official request. When deciding whether the evidence is in a foreign country, however, a lower standard applies: a court must 'find[] by a preponderance of the evidence ... that it *reasonably appears*, or reasonably appeared at the time the request was made, that such evidence is, or was, in a foreign country.' [§3292(a)(1)] (emphasis added). In other words, this element is satisfied even if the court itself is not certain that a preponderance of the evidence shows that the evidence is in a foreign country, so long as a reasonable factfinder could have come to that conclusion").

[66] *United States v. Trainor*, 376 F.3d 1325, 1330-335 (11th Cir. 2004); *United States v. Wilson*, 322 F.3d 353,363 (5th Cir. 2003); *DeGeorge v. U.S. District Court*, 219 F.3d 930, 937 (9th Cir. 2000).

[67] *United States v. Jenkins*, 633 F.3d 788, 798 (9th Cir. 2011), quoting, *United States v. Trainor*, 376 F.3d at 1332-33 ("[T]he government must meet a 'minimum evidentiary burden.' ... The government can satisfy its burden of proof under §3289(a)(1) 'by including a sworn or verified application containing the necessary factual information, testimony by Government officials, affidavits, declarations, exhibits, or other materials of evidentiary value,' even including hearsay evidence"); see also, *United States v. Little*, 667 F.3d at 224.

[68] *United States v. Little*, 667 F.3d at 224-25.

[69] *United States v. Atiyeh*, 402 F.3d 354, 362-63 (3d Cir. 2005).

[70] 18 U.S.C. 3292(b); *United States v. Jenkins*, 633 F.3d at 798-99.

[71] 18 U.S.C. 3292(b).

i.e., when the United States is satisfied its request has been answered;[72] yet at least one believes that final action occurs when the foreign government believes it has provided a final response.[73]

Fugitives

A provision exempting fugitives accompanied passage of the first federal statute of limitations.[74] The language has changed little since ("no statute of limitations shall extend to any person fleeing from justice," 18 U.S.C. 3290), but its meaning remains a topic of debate.[75] Most circuits, taking their lead from *Streep v. United States*, 160 U.S. 128 (1895), have held that the government must establish that the accused acted with an intent to avoid prosecution.[76] Yet two have held that mere absence from the jurisdiction is sufficient.[77] Even in the more demanding circuits, however, flight is thought to include the accused's concealing himself within the jurisdiction,[78] or remaining outside the jurisdiction when he becomes aware of the possibility of prosecution,[79] or fleeing before an investigation begins[80] or to avoid prosecution on another matter,[81] or to avoid civil or administrative justice rather than criminal justice.[82]

---

[72] *United States v. Bischel*, 61 F.3d 1429, 1432-434 (9th Cir. 1995); *United States v. Torres*, 318 F.3d 1058, 1061-65 (11th Cir. 2003).

[73] *Untied States v. Meador*, 138 F.3d 986, 991-94 (5th Cir. 1998).

[74] 1 Stat. 119 (1790)("nothing herein contained shall extend to any person or persons fleeing from justice").

[75] See generally, *What Constitutes "Fleeing From Justice" Within the Meaning of 18 U.S.C.A. §3290 Which Provides That No Statute of Limitations Shall Extend to Persons Fleeing From Justice*, 148 ALR FED 573.

[76] *Choe v. Torres*, 525 F.3d 733, 741 (9th Cir. 2008); *United States v. Gibson*, 490 F.3d 604, 608 (7th Cir. 2007); *United States v. Florez*, 447 F.3d 145, 150-51 (2d Cir. 2006); *Ross v. U.S. Marshal*, 168 F.3d 1190, 1193-194 (10th Cir. 1999); *United States v. Greever*, 134 F.3d 777, 780 (6th Cir. 1998); *United States v. Foseca-Machado*, 53 F.3d 1242, 1244 (11th Cir. 1995); *Donnell v. United States*, 229 F.2d 560, 565 (5th Cir. 1956); *Brouse v. United States*, 68 F.2d 294, 295 (1st Cir. 1933).

[77] *In re Assarsson*, 687 F.2d 1157, 1162 (8th Cir. 1982); *McGowen v. United States*, 105 F.2d 791, 792 (D.C. Cir. 1939). *Streep* declared that it "unnecessary, for the purposes of the present case, to undertake to give an exhaustive definition of these words [fleeing from justice]; for it is quite clear that any person who takes himself out of the jurisdiction, with the intention of avoiding being brought to justice for a particular offense, can have no benefit of the limitation, at least when prosecuted for that offense in a court of the United States," 160 U.S. at 133. In context, it might be thought unclear whether the Court meant flight with intent was required or merely sufficient.

[78] *United States v. Florez*, 447 F.3d at 152; *United States v. Greever*, 134 F.3d at 780.

[79] *United States v. Fowlie*, 24 F.3d 1070, 1072-73 (9th Cir. 1994); *United States v. Rivera-Ventura*, 72 F.3d 277, 283-84 (2d Cir. 1995); *United States v. Catino*, 735 F.2d 718, 722-23 (2d Cir. 1984).

[80] *Ross v. U.S. Marshal*, 168 F.3d at 1194-195.

[81] *United States v. Morgan*, 922 F.2d 1495, 1496-497 (10th Cir. 1991); *United States v. Rivera-Ventura*, 72 F.3d at 283; *United States v. Gonzalez*, 675 F.2d 1050, 1052-53 (9th Cir. 1982).

[82] *United States v. Rivera-Ventura*, 72 F.3d at 284.

Conspiracies and Continuing Offenses

Statutes of limitation "normally begin to run when the crime is complete"[83] which occurs when the last element of the crime has been satisfied.[84] The rule for conspiracy is a bit different.[85] The general conspiracy statute consists of two elements: (1) an agreement to commit a federal crime or to defraud the United States and (2) an overt act committed in furtherance of the agreement.[86] Conspirators left uninterrupted will frequently continue on through several overt acts to the ultimate commission of the underlying substantive offenses which are the objectives of their plots. Thus, the statute of limitations for such conspiracies runs not from the first overt act committed in furtherance of the conspiracy but from the last.[87] The statute of limitations under conspiracy statutes that have no overt act requirement runs from the accomplishment of the objectives of the conspiracy or from its abandonment.[88]

Concealment of the criminal plot after its completion is considered a natural component of all conspiracies. Consequently, overt acts of concealment after the objectives of the conspiracy have been accomplished may not be used to delay the running of the statute of limitations.[89] Overt acts of concealment which are among the original objectives of the conspiracy as charged in the

---

[83] *Toussie v. United States*, 397 U.S. 112, 115 (1970), quoting, *Pendergast v. United States*, 317 U.S. 412, 418 (1943); see also, *United States v. Venti*, 687 F.3d 501, 503 (1st Cir. 2012); *United States v. Eppolito*, 543 F.3d 25, 46 (2d Cir. 2008); *United States v. Reitmeyer*, 356 F.3d 1313, 1317 (10th Cir. 2004); *United States v. Najjor*, 255 F.3d 979, 983 (9th Cir. 2001); *United States v. Dees*, 215 F.3d 378, 380 (3d Cir. 2000); *United States v. Yashar*, 166 F.3d 873, 875 (7th Cir. 1999); *United States v. Lutz*, 154 F.3d 581, 586 (6th Cir. 1998); *United States v. Gilbert*, 136 F.3d 1451, 1453 (11th Cir. 1998); *United States v. Gomez*, 38 F.3d 1031, 1034 (8th Cir. 1994); *United States v. Blizzard*, 27 F.3d 100, 102 (4th Cir. 1994).

[84] *United States v. Reitmeyer*, 356 F.3d 1313, 1317 (10th Cir. 2004); *United States v. Carlson*, 235 F.3d 466, 470 (9th Cir. 2000); *United States v. Crossley*, 224 F.3d 847, 859 (6th Cir. 2000); *United States v. Yashar*, 166 F.3d at 875; *United States v. Vebeliunas*, 76 F.3d 1283, 1293 (2d Cir. 1996).

[85] *See generally, When Is Conspiracy Continuing Offense for Purposes of Statute of Limitations Under 18 USCS §3282*, 106 ALR FED. 616.

[86] "If two or more persons conspire either to commit any offense against the United States, or to defraud the United States, or any agency thereof in any manner or for any purpose, and one or more of such persons do any act to effect the object of the conspiracy, each shall be fined under this title or imprisoned not more than five years, or both.... " 18 U.S.C. 371.

[87] *Fiswick v. United States*, 329 U.S. 211, 216 (1946); see also, *United States v. Cunningham*, 679 F.3d 355, 374 (6th Cir. 2012); *United States v. Mueller*, 661 F.3d 338, 347 (8th Cir. 2011); *United States v. Wright*, 651 F.3d 764, 770 (7th Cir. 2011); *United States v. Bornman*, 559 F.3d 150, 153 (3d Cir. 2009); *United States v. Eppolito*, 543 F.3d 25, 47 (2d Cir. 2008); *United States v. Qayyum*, 451 F.3d 1214, 1218 (10th Cir. 2006); *United States v. Arias*, 431 F.3d 1327, 1340 (11th Cir. 2005)("if a conspirator establishes the affirmative defense of withdrawal, the statute of limitations [as to him] will begin to run at the time of withdrawal. Otherwise, the statute will not begin to run until the final act of the conspiracy has occurred"); *United States v. Hitt*, 349 F.3d 1010, 1015 (D.C.Cir. 2001); *United States v. Monaco*, 194 F.3d 381, 387 n.2 (2d Cir. 1999); *United States v. Manges*, 110 F.3d 1162, 1169 (5th Cir. 1997). Conspiracies live on as long as the conspirators continue to receive the economic benefits of the scheme, *United States v. Salmonese*, 352 F.3d 608, 614-17 (2d Cir. 2003).

[88] *United States v. Wilbur*, 674 F.3d 1160, 1176 (9th Cir. 2012); *United States v. Nunez*, 673 F.3d 661, 663 (7th Cir. 2012); *United States v. Fishman*, 645 F.3d 1175, 1191 (10th Cir. 2011); *United States v. McNair*, 605 F.3d 1152, 1213 (11th Cir. 2010); *United States v. Saadey*, 393 F.3d 669, 677 (6th Cir. 2005); *United States v. Therm-All, Inc.*, 373 F.3d 625, 632 (5th Cir. 2004); *United States v. Grimmett*, 236 F.3d 452, 453 (8th Cir. 2001); *United States v. Tocco*, 200 F.3d 401, 425 n.9 (6th Cir. 2000).

[89] *Grunewald v. United States*, 353 U.S. 391, 406 (1957); see also, *United States v. Qayyum*, 451 F.3d 1214, 1219 (10th Cir. 2006); *United States v. Grenoble*, 413 F.3d 569, 575-76 (6th Cir. 2005); *United States v. Arnold*, 117 F.3d 1308, 1314 (11th Cir. 1997); *United States v. Maloney*, 71 F.3d 645, 659 (7th Cir. 1995).

indictment, however, may serve as the point at which the statute of limitations begins to run.[90] Distinguishing between the two is sometimes difficult.

There are other crimes, which, like conspiracy, continue on long after all the elements necessary for their prosecution are first present. The applicable statute of limitations for these continuing crimes is delayed if either "the explicit language of the substantive criminal statute compels such a conclusion, or the nature of the crime involved is such that Congress must assuredly have intended that it be treated as a continuing one."[91] Continuing federal offenses for purposes of the statutes of limitation include:

- escape from federal custody, *United States v. Bailey*, 444 U.S. 394, 636 (1980);[92]
- flight to avoid prosecution, *United States v. Merino*, 44 F.3d 749, 753-54 (9th Cir. 1994);[93]
- failure to report for sentencing, *United States v. Gray*, 876 F.2d 1411, 1419 (9th Cir. 1989);[94]
- possession of the skin and skull of an endangered species, *United States v. Winnie*, 97 F.3d 975, 975-76 (7th Cir. 1996);[95]
- possession of counterfeit currency, *United States v. Kayfez*, 957 F.2d 677, 678 (9th Cir. 1992);[96]

---

[90] *Grunewald v. United States*, 353 U.S. at 406; *see also, United States v. Qayyum*, 451 F.3d 1214, 1219 (10th Cir. 2006); *United States v. Mann*, 161 F.3d 840, 859 (5th Cir. 1998); *United States v. Arnold*, 117 F.3d at 1314; *United States v. Maloney*, 71 F.3d at 659-60; *United States v. Rabinowitz*, 56 F.3d 932, 934 (8th Cir. 1995).

[91] *Toussie v. United States*, 397 U.S. at 115; *United States v. Smith*, 373 F.3d 561, 563-64 (4th Cir. 2004); *United States v. Reitmeyer*, 356 F.3d 1313, 1322 (10th Cir. 2004).

[92] "Whoever escapes or attempts to escape from the custody of the Attorney General or his authorized representative, or from any institution or facility in which he is confined by direction of the Attorney General, or from any custody under or by virtue of any process issued under the laws of the United States by any court, judge, or commissioner, or from the custody of an officer or employee of the United States pursuant to lawful arrest, shall, if the custody or confinement is by virtue of an arrest on a charge of felony, or conviction of any offense, be fined under this title or imprisoned not more than five years, or both; or if the custody or confinement is for extradition, or for exclusion or expulsion proceedings under the immigration laws, or by virtue of an arrest or charge of or for a misdemeanor, and prior to conviction, be fined under this title or imprisoned not more than one year, or both," 18 U.S.C. 751(a).

[93] "Whoever moves or travels in interstate or foreign commerce with intent either (1) to avoid prosecution, or custody or confinement after conviction, under the laws of the place from which he flees, for a crime, or an attempt to commit a crime, punishable by death or which is a felony under the laws of the place from which the fugitive flees, or (2) to avoid giving testimony in any criminal proceedings in such place in which the commission of an offense punishable by death or which is a felony under the laws of such place, is charged, or (3) to avoid service of, or contempt proceedings for alleged disobedience of, lawful process requiring attendance and the giving of testimony or the production of documentary evidence before an agency of a State empowered by the law of such State to conduct investigations of alleged criminal activities, shall be fined under this title or imprisoned not more than five years, or both...." 18 U.S.C. 1073.

[94] "Whoever, having been released under this chapter knowingly—(1) fails to appear before a court as required by the conditions of release; or (2) fails to surrender for service of sentence pursuant to a court order; shall be punished as provided in subsection (b) of this section," 18 U.S.C. 3146(a).

[95] "It is unlawful for any person subject to the jurisdiction of the United States to engage in any trade in any specimens contrary to the provisions of the Convention [on International Trade in Endangered Species], or to possess any specimens traded contrary to the provisions of the Convention, including the definitions of terms in article I thereof," 16 U.S.C. 1538(c)(1).

[96] "Whoever, with intent to defraud, passes, utters, publishes, or sells, or attempts to pass, utter, publish, or sell, or with like intent brings into the United States or keeps in possession or conceals any falsely made, forged, counterfeited, or (continued...)

- kidnaping, *United States v. Denny-Shaffer*, 2 F.3d 999, 1018-19 (10th Cir. 1993);[97]

- failure to register under the Foreign Agents Registration Act, *United States v. McGoff*, 831 F.2d 1071, 1071 (D.C.Cir. 1987);[98]

- failure to register under the Selective Service Act, *United States v. Kerley*, 838 F.2d 932, 935 (7th Cir. 1988);[99]

- being found in the United States having reentered this country after deportation, *United States v. Gomez*, 38 F.3d 1031, 1035 (8th Cir. 1994);[100]

- embezzlement under some circumstances, *United States v. Smith*, 373 F.3d 561, 568 (4th Cir. 2004);[101]

- possession of unregistered pipe bombs, *United States v. Berndt*, 530 F.3d 553, 554-55 (7th Cir. 2008);[102]

(...continued)
altered obligation or other security of the United States, shall be fined under this title or imprisoned not more than 15 years, or both," 18 U.S.C. 472.

[97] "(a) Whoever unlawfully seizes, confines, inveigles, decoys, kidnaps, abducts, or carries away and holds for ransom or reward or otherwise any person, except in the case of a minor by the parent thereof, when—(1) the person is willfully transported in interstate or foreign commerce, regardless of whether the person was alive when transported across a State boundary if the person was alive when the transportation began; (2) any such act against the person is done within the special maritime and territorial jurisdiction of the United States; (3) any such act against the person is done within the special aircraft jurisdiction of the United States as defined in section 46501 of Title 49; (4) the person is a foreign official, an internationally protected person, or an official guest as those terms are defined in section 1116(b) of this title; or (5) the person is among those officers and employees described in section 1114 of this title and any such act against the person is done while the person is engaged in, or on account of, the performance of official duties; shall be punished by imprisonment for any term of years or for life and, if the death of any person results, shall be punished by death or life imprisonment," 18 U.S.C. 1201(a); *see also, United States v. Garcia*, 854 F.2d 340, 343 (9th Cir. 1988)(the statute of limitations does not begin to run until the victim is released); if the victim is killed, the offense is a capital crime and the prosecution may be brought at any time.

[98] "Failure to file any such registration statement or supplements thereto as is required by either section 612(a) or section 612(b) of this title [relating to registration requirements] shall be considered a continuing offense for as long as such failure exists, notwithstanding any statute of limitation or other statute to the contrary ," 22 U.S.C. 618(e).

[99] "No person shall be prosecuted, tried, or punished for evading, neglecting, or refusing to perform the duty of registering imposed by Section 3 of this title [Section 453 of this Appendix] unless the indictment is found within five years next after the last day before such person attains the age of twenty-six, or within five years next after the last day before such person does perform his duty to register, whichever shall first occur," 50 U.S.C.App. 462(d); *see also, United States v. Jacob*, 781 F.2d 643, 648-49 (8th Cir. 1986).

[100] "Subject to subsection (b) of this section, any alien who—(1) has been denied admission, excluded, deported, or removed or has departed the United States while an order of exclusion, deportation, or removal is outstanding, and thereafter (2) enters, attempts to enter, or is at any time found in, the United States, unless (A) prior to his reembarkation at a place outside the United States or his application for admission from foreign contiguous territory, the Attorney General has expressly consented to such alien's reapplying for admission; or (B) with respect to an alien previously denied admission and removed, unless such alien shall establish that he was not required to obtain such advance consent under this chapter or any prior Act, shall be fined under Title 18, or imprisoned not more than two years, or both," 8 U.S.C. 1326(a); *see also, United States v. Santana-Castellano*, 74 F.3d 593, 597 (5th Cir. 1996)("Likewise, the five year statute of limitations under Sec. 1326 begins to run at the time the alien is found barring circumstances that suggest that the INS should have known of his presence earlier, such as when he reentered the United States through an official border checkpoint in the good faith belief that his entry was legal"); *United States v. DiSantillo*, 615 F.2d 128, 132 (3d Cir. 1980).

[101] "We believe that the specific conduct at issue here is more properly characterized as a continuing offense rather than a series of separate acts. The facts found by the district court were sufficient to prove that he set into place and maintained an automatically recurring scheme whereby funds were electronically deposited in his account and retained for his own use without need for any specific action on his part," *Id.*

- failure to pay child support, *United States v. Edelkind*, 525 F.3d 388, 393-94 (5th Cir. 2008);[103] and

- possession of an immigration document obtained fraudulently, *United States v. Krstic*, 558 F.3d 1010, 1017-18 (9th Cir. 2009).[104]

Constitutional Considerations

Constitutional challenges to the application of various statutes of limitation perhaps most often claim support from the ex post facto or due process clauses. The Constitution prohibits both Congress and the states from enacting ex post facto laws.[105] More precisely it prohibits:

> 1st. Every law that makes an action done before the passing of the law, and which was innocent when done, criminal; and punishes such action. 2d. Every law that aggravates a crime, or makes it greater than it was, when committed. 3d. Every law that changes the punishment, and inflicts a greater punishment, than the law annexed to the crime, when committed. 4th. Every law that alters the legal rules of evidence, and receives less, or different, testimony, than the law required at the time of the commission of the offense, in order to convict the offender.[106]

The lower federal appellate courts had long felt that a statute that extends a period of limitation before its expiration did not offend the ex post facto clauses, but that the clauses ban laws that attempt to revive and extend an expired statute of limitations.[107] Until the United States Supreme

---

(...continued)

[102] "It shall be unlawful for any person ... (d) to receive or possess a firearm which is not registered to him in the National Firearms Registration and Transfer Record...." 26 U.S.C. 5861(d); "For the purpose of this chapter ... (a) ... The term 'firearm' means ... (8) a destructive device.... (f) ... The term 'destructive device' means (1) any explosive, incendiary, or poison gas (A) bomb,...." 26 U.S.C. 5845(d)(8), (f)(1).

[103] "Any person who - (1) willfully fails to pay a support obligation with respect to a child who resides in another State, if such obligation has remained unpaid for a period longer than 1 year, or is greater than $5,000; (2) travels in interstate or foreign commerce with the intent to evade a support obligation, if such obligation has remained unpaid for a period longer than 1 year, or is greater than $5,000; or (3) willfully fails to pay a support obligation with respect to a child who resides in another State, if such obligation has remained unpaid for a period longer than 2 years, or is greater than $10,000; shall be punished as provided in subsection (c)." 18 U.S.C. 228(a).

[104] "Whoever knowingly forges, counterfeits, alters, or falsely makes any immigrant or nonimmigrant visa, permit, border crossing card, alien registration receipt card, or other document prescribed by statute or regulation for entry into or as evidence of authorized stay or employment in the United States, or utters, uses, attempts to use, *possesses*, obtains, accepts, or receives any such visa, permit, border crossing card, alien registration receipt card, or other document prescribed by statute or regulation for entry into or as evidence of authorized stay or employment in the United States, knowing it to be forged, counterfeited, altered, or falsely made, or to have been procured by means of any false claim or statement, or to have been otherwise procured by fraud or unlawfully obtained.... Shall be fined under this title or imprisoned not more than...." 18 U.S.C. 1546(a).

[105] "No Bill of Attainder or ex post facto Law shall be passed.... No State shall ... pass any Bill of Attainder, [or] ex post facto Law.... U.S. Const. Art. I, §§9, 10.

[106] *Stogner v. California*, 539 U.S. 607, 612 (2003), quoting, *Calder v. Bull,* 3 Dall. (3 U.S.) 386, 390 (1798) (*seriatim* opinion of Chase, J.).

[107] *United States v. De La Mata*, 266 F.3d 1275, 1286 (11th Cir. 2001); *United States v. Grimes*, 142 F.3d 1342, 1351 (11th Cir. 1998); *United States v. Morrow*, 177 F.3d 272, 294 (5th Cir. 1999); *United States v. Chandler*, 66 F.3d 1460, 1467 (8th Cir. 1995); *United States v. Taliaferro*, 979 F.2d 1399, 1402-403 (10th Cir. 1992); *United States v. Knipp*, 963 F.2d 839, 844 (6th Cir. 1992); *United States ex rel. Massarella v. Elrod*, 682 F.2d 688, 689 (7th Cir. 1982); *United States v. Richardson*, 512 F.2d 105, 196 (3d Cir. 1975); *United States v. Clemens*, 266 F.2d 397, 399 (9th Cir. 1959); *Falter v. United States*, 23 F.2d 420, 425-26 (2d Cir. 1928).

Court confirmed that view in *Stogner v. California*,[108] however, there were well regarded contrary opinions. The California Supreme Court, for example, at one point concluded that the ex post facto clauses in fact pose no impediment to the revival of an expired statute of limitations.[109] The Justice Department cited the California case, *Frazer*, in its summary of proposed anti-terrorism legislation,[110] suggesting that its retroactive section was intended both to extend the statutes of limitation to cases where the period of limitation had not run and to revive the prospect of prosecution where the period had expired. The USA PATRIOT Act's retroactivity clause used the same language found in the Justice Department's original proposal,[111] arguably reflecting the same intent.

The California court, however, had read too much into then contemporary United States Supreme Court interpretations of the ex post facto clause. *Frazer* involved a statutory amendment which allowed prosecution of certain child sex offense cases within one year after the offense had been reported to authorities even if the otherwise applicable statute of limitations had run. The *Frazer* court pointed out that the Supreme Court had apparently pruned its *Calder* statement so as to define ex post facto laws as "any statute which punishes as a crime an act previously committed, which was innocent when done; which makes more burdensome the punishment for a crime, after its commission, or which deprives one charged with crime of any defenses available according to law at the time when the act was committed." [112] Moreover, as the California court understood it, the Supreme Court had not only indicated that evidentiary changes were beyond the realm of the clauses' protection but that the defenses protected by the clauses were limited to those based on the elements or punishment of the crime when it was committed.[113]

The Supreme Court subsequently warned that *Collins* should not be read as a repudiation of *Calder's* four prohibited classes, but instead that "*Collins* held that it was a mistake to stray *beyond Calder's* four categories." [114] The Court seemed to further signal its reluctance to reach beyond the limits of *Calder* when it declined to extend the ex post facto proscription to cover a retroactive application of a judicial (rather than a legislative) change in the law.[115] These

---

[108] 539 U.S. 607 (2003).

[109] *People v. Frazer*, 24 Cal.4th 737, 759, 982 P.2d 180, 194, 88 Cal.Rptr.2d 312, 327 (1999).

[110] *Section 301. No Statute of Limitations For Prosecuting Terrorism Offenses, Consultation Draft of September 20, 2001, Anti-Terrorism Act of 2001, Section-by-Section Analysis*, printed in, *Administration's Draft Anti-Terrorism Act of 2001: Hearing Before the House Comm. on the Judiciary*, 107th Cong., 1st Sess. 60 (2001)("This section expressly provides that it is applicable to offenses committed before the date of enactment of the statute, as well as those committed thereafter.... The constitutionality of such retroactive applications of changes in statutes of limitation is well settled. See, e.g., *United States v. Grimes*, 142 F.3d 1342, 1350-51 (11th Cir. 1998); *People v. Frazer*, 982 P.2d 180 (Cal. 1999)"). *Grimes* cited the earlier lower federal case law and declared, "We now join our fellow circuits in holding that application of a statute of limitations extended before the original limitations period has expired does not violate the ex post facto clause," 142 F.3d at 1351. Note that *Grimes* said nothing of cases reviving the possibility of prosecution *after* the original limitations period had expired.

[111] "The amendments made by this section shall apply to the prosecution of any offense committed before, on, or after the date of the enactment of this section,"§809(b), P.L. 107-56, 115 Stat. 272, 380 (2001); *Section 301(c). No Statute of Limitations For Prosecuting Terrorism Offenses*, H.R._____ , *Anti-Terrorism Act of 2001*, printed in, *Administration's Draft Anti-Terrorism Act of 2001: Hearing Before the House Comm. on the Judiciary*, 107th Cong., 1st Sess. 82 (2001). This same text appeared in the version of the bill reported out of the House Judiciary Committee, §301(c), H.R. 2975, reprinted in H.Rept. 107-236, at 26 (2001).

[112] 21 Cal.4th at 755, 982 at 191, 88 Cal.Rptr.2d at 324, *quoting, Beazell v. Ohio*, 269 U.S. 167, 169 (1925).

[113] 21 Cal.4th at 755-57, 982 at191-92, 88 Cal.Rptr.2d at 324-26, *citing, Collins v. Youngblood*, 497 U.S. 37, 43 n.3, 50 (1990).

[114] *Carmell v. Texas*, 529 U.S. 513, 539 (2000)(emphasis in the original).

[115] "Justice Scalia makes much of the fact that at the time of the framing of the Constitution, it was widely accepted ... (continued...)

developments did not necessarily undermine the California decision in *Frazer*, however, since its revival of a statute of limitations that had run did not appear to fit easily within any of the *Calder* categories. But the *Frazer* analysis was in error nonetheless.

The U.S. Supreme Court in *Stogner* characterized the California legislative revival of an expired period of limitation as not only "manifestly unjust and oppressive," but among those laws that run afoul of *Calder's* second standard ("Every law that aggravates a crime, or makes it greater than it was, when committed").[116] As properly understood and alternatively characterized in *Calder*, this second category embraces statutes that like the California statute "inflicted punishments, where the party was not by law, liable to any punishment," at the time.[117]

Retroactivity aside, the due process clauses may be implicated if a crime is not subject to any statute of limitations or if the period of limitation has not run. Although statutes of limitation alone generally govern the extent of permissible pre-indictment delay, extraordinary circumstances may trigger due process implications. The Supreme Court in *Marion* observed that even "the Government concedes that the Due Process Clause of the Fifth Amendment would require dismissal of [an] indictment if it were shown at trial that the pre-indictment delay ... caused substantial prejudice to [a defendant's] rights to a fair trial and that the delay was an intentional device to gain tactical advantage over the accused."[118] The Court declined to dismiss the indictment there, however, because the defendants failed to show they had suffered any actual prejudice from the delay or to show "that the Government intentionally delayed to gain some tactical advantage over [them] or to harass them."[119]

The Court later made clear that due process contemplates more than a claimant's showing of adverse impact caused by pre-indictment delay: "Thus *Marion* makes clear that proof of prejudice is generally a necessary but not sufficient element of a due process claim, and that the due process inquiry must consider the reasons for the delay as well as the prejudice to the accused."[120]

(...continued)
that (according to Justice Scalia) there is no doubt that the ex post facto clause would have prohibited a legislative decision identical to the Tennessee court's decision here. This latter argument seeks at bottom merely to reopen what has long been settled by the constitutional text and our own decisions: that the ex post facto clause does not apply to judicial decisions," *Rogers v. Tennessee*, 532 U.S. 451, 462 (2001). The case arose when the Tennessee Supreme Court abrogated a previous common law rule that barred a murder prosecution unless the victim died within a year and a day of the defendant's assault upon the victim.

[116] *Stogner v. California*, 539 U.S. 607, 611-12 (2003).

[117] *Id.* at 612, *quoting*, *Calder*, 3 Dall. (3 U.S.) at 389.

[118] *United States v. Marion*, 404 U.S. 307, 324 (1971); *see also*, *United States v. Gouveia*, 467 U.S. 180, 192 (1984)("But applicable statutes of limitations protect against the prosecution's bringing stale criminal charges against any defendant, and, beyond that protection, the Fifth Amendment requires the dismissal of an indictment, even if it is brought within the statute of limitations, if the defendant can prove that the Government's delay in bringing the indictment was a deliberate device to gain an advantage over him and that it caused him actual prejudice in presenting his defense").

[119] *United States v. Marion*, 404 U.S. at 325.

[120] *United States v. Lovasco*, 431 U.S. 783, 790 (1977); *see also*, *Arizona v. Youngblood*, 488 U.S. 51, 57 (1988) ("Our decisions in related areas have stressed the importance for constitutional purposes of good or bad faith on the part of the Government when the claim is based on the loss of evidence attributable to the Government").

Perhaps because so few defendants have been able to show sufficient prejudice to necessitate further close inquiry,[121] the lower federal appellate courts seem at odds over exactly what else due process demands before it will require dismissal. Most have held that the defendant bears the burden of establishing both prejudice and government deficiency;[122] others that once the defendant establishes prejudice the burden shifts to the government to negate the second prong;[123] and still others that once the defendant shows prejudice the court must balance the harm against the justifications for delay.[124]

---

[121] This initial burden has been described as heavy and rarely met, *United States v. Gilbert*, 266 F.3d 1180, 1187 (9th Cir. 2001); *United States v. Cornielle*, 171 F.3d 748, 752 (2d Cir. 1999). The defendant must show more than mere speculative harm; he "must specifically identify witnesses or documents lost during the delay properly attributable to the government, relate the substance of the testimony which would have been offered by the missing witnesses or the information contained in lost documents in sufficient detail to permit a court to assess accurately whether the information was material to his defense, and show that the missing testimony or other evidence is not available from alternative sources," *United States v. Al-Muqsit*, 191 F.3d 928, 938 (8th Cir. 1999); *see also, United States v. Beckman*, 183 F.3d 891, 895 (8th Cir. 1999); *United States v. Trammell*, 133 F.3d 1343, 1351 (10th Cir. 1998); *United States v. Crouch*, 84 F.3d 1497, 1514-516 (5th Cir. 1996).

[122] *United States v. Madden*, 682 F.3d 920, 929 (10th Cir. 2012)("Preindictment delay is not a violation of the Due Process Clause unless the defendant shows both that the delay caused actual prejudice and that the government delayed purposefully in order to gain a tactical advantage"); *United States v. Wetherald*, 636 F.3d 1315, 1324 (11th Cir. 2011) (internal citations omitted)("To establish that a pre-indictment delay violated his due process rights, a defendant must show (1) that he was actually prejudiced by the delay in preparing his defense, and (2) the delay was unreasonable. We look at unreasonableness in pre-indictment delay cases through the lens of tactical advantage, and the court has said that the motivations behind the delay must violate fundamental conceptions of justice, or a sense of fair play or decency"); *United States v. Seale*, 600 F.3d 473, 479 (5th Cir. 2010)("To show an unconstitutional pre-indictment delay, a party must establish two elements; 1) the Government intended to delay obtaining an indictment for the purpose of gaining some tactical advantage over the accused in the contemplated prosecution or for some other bad faith purpose, and 2) that the improper delay caused actual, substantial prejudice to his defense"); *United States v. Bater*, 594 F.3d 51, 54 (1st Cir. 2010); *United States v. Schaffer*, 586 F.3d 414,424 (6th Cir. 2009); *United States v. Uribe-Rios*, 558 F.3d 347, 358 (4th Cir. 2009); *United States v. Corona-Verbera*, 509 F.3d 1105, 1112 (9th Cir. 2007*)* ("In order to succeed on his claim that he was denied due process because of pre-indictment delay, Corona-Verbera must satisfy both prongs of a two-part test. First, he must prove actual, nonspeculative prejudice from the delay. Second, the length of the delay is weighed against the reasons for the delay, and Corona-Verbera must show that the delay offends those fundamental conceptions of justice which lie at the base of our civil and political institutions"); *United States v. Galdney*, 474 F.3d 1027, 1030 (8th Cir. 2007); *United States v. Beckett*, 208 F.3d 140, 150 (3d Cir. 2000).

[123] *United States v. Henderson*, 337 F.3d 914, 920 (7th Cir. 2003); *United States v. McMutuary*, 217 F.3d 477, 481 (7th Cir. 2000); *United States v. Spears*, 159 F.3d 1081, 1084 (7th Cir. 1999); *United States v. Benshop*, 138 F.3d 1229, 1232 (8th Cir. 1998).

[124] *United States v. Barken*, 412 F.3d 1131, 1134 (9th Cir. 2005); *United States v. Al-Muqsit*, 191 F.3d 928, 938 (8th Cir. 1999); *United States v. McDougal*, 133 F.3d 1110, 1113 (8th Cir. 1998); *United States v. Ross*, 123 F.3d 1181, 1184 (9th Cir. 1997); *Jones v. Angelone*, 94 F.3d 900, 904 (4th Cir. 1996); *see also, United States v. DeGeorge*, 380 F.3d 1203, 1210-211 (9th Cir. 2004)(internal quotation marks omitted)("DeGeorge must satisfy a two-part test to establish that pre-indictment delay has violated his due process rights: 1) he must prove that he suffered actual, non-speculative prejudice from the delay; and 2) he must show that the delay when balanced against the government's reasons for it, offends those fundamental conceptions of justice which lie at the base of our civil and political institutions").

Appendix A. Periods of Limitation for Specific Federal Crimes

No limitation

1. *Capital Offenses*

7 U.S.C. 2146(b) (killing federal employee engaged in duties with respect to transportation and sale of certain animals)

8 U.S.C. 1324 (1) (bringing in or harboring aliens where death results)

15 U.S.C. 1825(a)(2)(C) (killing those enforcing the Horse Protection Act)

18 U.S.C. 32, 33, 34 (destruction of aircraft, commercial motor vehicles or their facilities where death results)

18 U.S.C. 36 (drive-by shooting resulting in 1st degree murder)

18 U.S.C. 37 (violence at international airports where death results)

18 U.S.C. 43, 3559(f) (animal enterprise terrorism constituting murder of a child)

18 U.S.C. 115 (kidnaping with death resulting of the member of the family of a federal official or employee to obstruct or retaliate)

18 U.S.C. 115 (1st degree murder of the member of the family of a federal official or employee to obstruct or retaliate)

18 U.S.C. 175 (development or possession of biological weapons)

18 U.S.C. 175c, 3559(f) (variola virus offense constituting murder of a child)

18 U.S.C. 229, 229A (use of chemical weapons where death results)

18 U.S.C. 241 (conspiracy against civil rights where death results)

18 U.S.C. 242 (deprivation civil rights under color of law where death results)

18 U.S.C. 245 (discriminatory obstruction of enjoyment of federal protected activities where death results)

18 U.S.C. 247 (obstruction of the exercise of religious beliefs where death results)

18 U.S.C. 249 (hate crime resulting in death)

18 U.S.C. 351 (1st degree murder of a Member of Congress)

18 U.S.C. 351 (conspiracy to kill or kidnap a Member of Congress if death results)

18 U.S.C. 351 (kidnaping a Member of Congress if death results)

18 U.S.C. 794 (espionage)

18 U.S.C. 831, 3559(f) (nuclear material offense constituting murder of a child)

18 U.S.C. 844(d) (use of fire or explosives unlawfully where death results)

18 U.S.C. 844(f)(burning or bombing federal property where death results)

18 U.S.C. 844(i)(burning or bombing property affecting interstate commerce where death results)

18 U.S.C. 924(j)(1) (murder while in possession of a firearm during the commission of a crime of violence or drug trafficking)

18 U.S.C. 930(c) (1st degree murder while in possession of a firearm in a federal building)

18 U.S.C. 1091 (genocide where death results)

18 U.S.C. 1111 (1st degree murder within the special maritime or territorial jurisdiction of the U.S.)

18 U.S.C. 1121(b) (killing a state law enforcement officer by a federal prisoner or while transferring a prisoner interstate)

18 U.S.C. 1114 (1st degree murder of a federal officer or employee)

18 U.S.C. 1116 (1st degree murder of a foreign dignitary)

18 U.S.C. 1118 (murder by a federal prisoner)

18 U.S.C. 1119 (1st degree murder of an American by an American overseas)

18 U.S.C. 1120 (1st degree murder by an escaped federal prisoner)

18 U.S.C. 1121 (1st degree murder of one assisting in a federal criminal investigation)

18 U.S.C. 1201 (kidnaping where death results)

18 U.S.C. 1203 (hostage taking where death results)

18 U.S.C. 1365, 3559(f) (tampering with consumer products constituting murder of a child)

18 U.S.C. 1503 (1st degree murder committed to obstruction of federal judicial proceedings)

18 U.S.C. 1512 (tampering with a federal witness or informant involving murder)

18 U.S.C. 1513 (retaliating against a federal witness or informant involving murder)

18 U.S.C. 1591, 2245 (murder committed during the course of sex trafficking by force, fraud or of a child)

18 U.S.C. 1651, 1652, 3559(f) (piracy involving murder of a child)

18 U.S.C. 1716 (mailing injurious articles with intent to injure or damage property where death results)

18 U.S.C. 1751 (kidnaping the President where death results)

18 U.S.C. 1751 (conspiracy to kill or kidnap the President where death results)

18 U.S.C. 1751 (1st degree murder of the President)

18 U.S.C. 1952, 3559(f) (travel in aid of racketeering involve the murder of child)

18 U.S.C. 1958 (use of interstate facilities in furtherance of a murder-for-hire where death results)

18 U.S.C. 1959 (murder in aid of racketeering activity)

18 U.S.C. 1992 (terrorist attacks on trains and mass transit)

18 U.S.C. 2113(e) (robbing a federally insured bank if death results)

18 U.S.C. 2118, 3559(f) (robbery or burglary involving controlled substances constituting murder of a child)

18 U.S.C. 2119 (carjacking where death results)

18 U.S.C. 2199, 3559(f) (murder of a child by a stowaway)

18 U.S.C. 2241, 2245 (aggravated sexual assault of a child under 12 years of age in the special maritime or territorial jurisdiction of the U.S. where death results)

18 U.S.C. 2242, 2245 (coercing or enticing interstate travel for sexual purposes where death results)

18 U.S.C. 2243, 2245 (transporting minors for sexual purposes resulting in the death of a child under 14 years of age)

18 U.S.C. 2244, 2245 (abusive sexual contact where death results)

18 U.S.C. 2251 (sexual exploitation of children where death results)

18 U.S.C. 2251A, 2245 (selling or buying children where death results)

18 U.S.C. 2260, 2245 (production of material depicting sexually explicit activities of a child where death results)

18 U.S.C. 2261, 2261A, 2262, 3559(f) (murder of a child involved in interstate domestic violence, stalking, or interstate violation of a protective order)

18 U.S.C. 2280 (violence against maritime navigation where death results)

18 U.S.C. 2281 (violence against maritime fixed platform where death results)

18 U.S.C. 2282A (interference with maritime commerce where death results)

18 U.S.C. 2283 (transportation of explosive, nuclear, chemical, biological or radioactive material resulting in death)

18 U.S.C. 2291 (destruction of a vessel or maritime facility)

18 U.S.C. 2332 (terrorist murder of an American outside the U.S.)

18 U.S.C. 2332a (use of weapons of mass destruction where death results)

18 U.S.C. 2332b (acts of terrorism transcending national boundaries where death results)

18 U.S.C. 2332f (bombing public places)

18 U.S.C. 2332g, 3559(f) (anti-aircraft missile offense constituting murder of a child)

18 U.S.C. 2332h, 3559(f) (radiological dispersal device offense constituting murder of a child)

18 U.S.C. 2340A (torture where death results)

18 U.S.C. 2381 (treason)

18 U.S.C. 2441 (war crimes where death results)

18 U.S.C. 2421, 2245 (transportation of illicit sexual purposes where death results)

18 U.S.C. 2422, 2245 (coercion or inducement to travel for illicit sexual purposes where death results)

18 U.S.C. 2423, 2245 (transportation of minors for illicit sexual purposes where death results)

18 U.S.C. 2425, 2245 (interstate transportation of information concerning a minor where death results)

21 U.S.C. 461 (killing a poultry inspector)

21 U.S.C. 675 (killing a meat inspector)

21 U.S.C. 848(c), 3591(b) (major drug kingpin violations)

21 U.S.C. 848(e)(1) (killing in furtherance of a serious drug trafficking violation or killing a law enforcement official in furtherance of a controlled substance violation)

21 U.S.C. 1041(c) (murder of an egg inspector)

42 U.S.C. 2000e-13 (murder of EEOC personnel)

42 U.S.C. 2283 (murder of federal nuclear inspectors)

49 U.S.C. 46502 (air piracy where death results)

49 U.S.C. 46506 (murder in the special aircraft jurisdiction of the United States)

2. *Terrorism-Related Offenses Resulting in or Involving the Risk of Death or Serious Injury*

18 U.S.C. 32 (destruction of aircraft or aircraft facilities)

18 U.S.C. 37 (violence at international airports)

18 U.S.C. 81 (arson within special maritime and territorial jurisdiction)

18 U.S.C. 175 or 175b (biological weapons offenses)

18 U.S.C. 175c (variola virus)

18 U.S.C. 229 (chemical weapons offenses)

18 U.S.C. 351(a),(b),(c), or (d) (congressional, cabinet, and Supreme Court assassination and kidnaping)

18 U.S.C. 831 (nuclear materials offenses)

18 U.S.C. 832 (participation in a foreign atomic weapons program)

18 U.S.C. 842(m) or (n) (plastic explosives offenses)

18 U.S.C. 844(f)(2) or (3)(arson and bombing of federal property risking or causing death)

18 U.S.C. 844(i) (burning or bombing of property used in, or used in activities affecting, commerce)

18 U.S.C. 930(c) (killing or attempted killing during an attack on a federal facility with a dangerous weapon)

18 U.S.C. 956(a)(1) (conspiracy to murder, kidnap, or maim persons abroad)

18 U.S.C. 1030(a)(1) (protection of computer systems containing classified information)

18 U.S.C. 1030(a)(5)(A)(i) (resulting in damage defined in 1030(a)(5)(B)(ii) through (v) (protection of computers)

18 U.S.C. 1114 (protection of officers and employees of the United States),

18 U.S.C. 1116 (murder or manslaughter of foreign officials, official guests, or internationally protected persons)

18 U.S.C. 1203 (hostage taking)

18 U.S.C. 1361 (destruction of federal property)

18 U.S.C. 1362 (destruction of communication lines, stations, or systems)

18 U.S.C. 1363 (injury to buildings or property within special maritime and territorial jurisdiction of the United States)

18 U.S.C. 1366(a) (destruction of energy facilities)

18 U.S.C. 1751(a),(b),(c), or (d) (Presidential and Presidential staff assassination and kidnaping)

18 U.S.C. 1992 (terrorist attacks on trains and mass transit)

18 U.S.C. 2155 (destruction of national defense materials, premises, or utilities),

18 U.S.C. 2156 (production of defective national defense material)

18 U.S.C. 2280 (violence against maritime navigation)

18 U.S.C. 2281 (violence against maritime fixed platforms)

18 U.S.C. 2332 (certain homicides and other violence against United States nationals occurring outside of the United States)

18 U.S.C. 2332a (use of weapons of mass destruction)

18 U.S.C. 2332b (acts of terrorism transcending national boundaries)

18 U.S.C. 2332f (bombing public places)

18 U.S.C. 2332g (anti-aircraft missiles)

18 U.S.C. 2332h (radiological dispersal devices)

18 U.S.C. 2339 (harboring terrorists)

18 U.S.C. 2339A (providing material support to terrorists)

18 U.S.C. 2339B (providing material support to terrorist organizations)

18 U.S.C. 2339C (financing terrorism)

18 U.S.C. 2339D (receipt of military training from a foreign terrorist organization)

18 U.S.C. 2340A (torture committed under color of law)

21 U.S.C. 960A (narcoterrorism)

42 U.S.C. 2122 (atomic weapons)

42 U.S.C. 2284 (sabotage of nuclear facilities or fuel)

49 U.S.C. 46502 (aircraft piracy)

49 U.S.C. 46504 (second sentence)(assault on a flight crew with a dangerous weapon)

49 U.S.C. 46505(b)(3) or (c) (explosive or incendiary devices, or endangerment of human life by means of weapons, or aircraft)

49 U.S.C. 46506 (if homicide or attempted homicide involved, application of certain criminal laws to acts on aircraft)

49 U.S.C. 60123(b) (destruction of interstate gas or hazardous liquid pipeline facility)

3. *Child Abduction and Sex Offenses*

18 U.S.C. 1201 (kidnaping a child)

18 U.S.C. 1591 (sex trafficking by force, fraud or of a child)

18 U.S.C. ch.109A

    18 U.S.C. 2241 (aggravated sexual abuse)

    18 U.S.C. 2242 (sexual abuse)

18 U.S.C. 2243 (sexual abuse of a ward or child)

18 U.S.C. 2244 (abusive sexual contact)

18 U.S.C. 2245 (sexual abuse resulting in death)

18 U.S.C. 2250 (failure to register as a sex offender)

18 U.S.C. ch. 110

18 U.S.C. 2251 (sexual exploitation of children)

18 U.S.C. 2251A (selling or buying children)

18 U.S.C. 2252 (transporting, distributing or selling child sexually exploitive material)

18 U.S.C. 2252A (transporting or distributing child pornography)

18 U.S.C. 2252B (misleading names on the Internet)

18 U.S.C. 2260 (making child sexually exploitative material overseas for export to the U.S.)

18 U.S.C. ch. 117

18 U.S.C. 2421 (transportation of illicit sexual purposes)

18 U.S.C. 2422 (coercing or enticing travel for illicit sexual purposes)

18 U.S.C. 2423 (travel involving illicit sexual activity with a child)

18 U.S.C. 2424 (filing false immigration statement)

18 U.S.C. 2425 (interstate transmission of information about a child relating to illicit sexual activity)

20 years

18 U.S.C. 668 (major art theft)

10 years

8 U.S.C. 1324(a) (harboring illegal aliens)

18 U.S.C. 81 (arson in the special maritime or territorial jurisdiction of the United States)

18 U.S.C. 215 (receipt by financial institution officials of commissions or gifts for procuring loans)

18 U.S.C. 656 (theft, embezzlement, or misapplication by bank officer or employee)

18 U.S.C. 657 (embezzlement by lending, credit and insurance institution officers or employees)

18 U.S.C. 844(f) (burning or bombing federal property)

18 U.S.C. 844(h) (carrying explosives during the commission of a federal offense or using fire or explosives to commit a federal offense)

18 U.S.C. 844 (i) (burning or bombing property used in or used in activities affecting commerce)

18 U.S.C. 1005 (fraud concerning bank entries, reports and transactions)

18 U.S.C. 1006 (fraud concerning federal credit institution entries, reports and transactions)

18 U.S.C. 1007 (fraud concerning Federal Deposit Insurance Corporation transactions)

18 U.S.C. 1014 (fraud concerning loan and credit applications generally; renewals and discounts; crop insurance)

18 U.S.C. 1033 (crimes by or affecting persons engaged in the business of insurance)

18 U.S.C. 1344 (bank fraud)

18 U.S.C. 1341 (mail fraud affecting a financial institution)

18 U.S.C. 1343 (wire fraud affecting a financial institution)

18 U.S.C. 1423 (misuse of evidence of citizenship or naturalization) (or conspiracy to commit)

18 U.S.C. 1424 (personation or misuse of papers in naturalization proceedings) (or conspiracy to commit)

18 U.S.C. 1425 (procurement of citizenship or naturalization unlawfully) (or conspiracy to commit)

18 U.S.C. 1426 (reproduction of naturalization or citizenship papers) (or conspiracy to commit)

18 U.S.C. 1427 (sale of naturalization or citizenship papers) (or conspiracy to commit)

18 U.S.C. 1428 (surrender of canceled naturalization certificate) (or conspiracy to commit)

18 U.S.C. 1541 (passport or visa issuance without authority) (or conspiracy to commit)

18 U.S.C. 1542 (false statement in application and use of passport) (or conspiracy to commit)

18 U.S.C. 1543 (forgery or false use of passport) (or conspiracy to commit)

18 U.S.C. 1544 (misuse of passport) (or conspiracy to commit)

18 U.S.C. 1581 (peonage; obstruction of justice)

18 U.S.C. 1583 (enticement into slavery)

18 U.S.C. 1584 (sale into involuntary servitude)

18 U.S.C. 1589 (forced labor)

18 U.S.C. 1590 (slave trafficking)

18 U.S.C. 1592 (document offenses involving slave trafficking)

18 U.S.C. 1963 (RICO violation involving bank fraud)

18 U.S.C. 2442 (recruiting or using child soldiers)

42 U.S.C. 2274 (communication of restricted data)

42 U.S.C. 2275 (receipt of restricted data)

42 U.S.C. 2276 (tampering with restricted data)

50 U.S.C. 783 (disclosure of classified information (with suspension until the end of any federal employment of the accused))

8 years

1. Generally

18 U.S.C. 32 (destruction of aircraft or aircraft facilities)

18 U.S.C. 37 (violence at international airports)

18 U.S.C. 112 (assaults upon diplomats)

18 U.S.C. 175 or 175b (biological weapons offenses)

18 U.S.C. 228 (chemical weapons offenses)

18 U.S.C. 351 (congressional, cabinet, and Supreme Court assassination, kidnaping, or assault)

18 U.S.C. 831 (nuclear materials offenses)

18 U.S.C. 842(m) or (n) (plastic explosives offenses)

18 U.S.C. 930(c) (killing or attempted killing during an attack on a federal facility with a dangerous weapon)

18 U.S.C. 956(a)(1) (conspiracy to murder, kidnap, or maim persons abroad)

18 U.S.C. 1030(a)(1) (protection of computer systems containing classified information)

18 U.S.C. 1030(a)(5)(A)(damaging certain computers)

18 U.S.C. 1114 (protection of officers and employees of the United States)

18 U.S.C. 1116 (murder or manslaughter of foreign officials, official guests, or internationally protected persons)

18 U.S.C. 1203 (hostage taking)

18 U.S.C. 1361 (destruction of federal property)

18 U.S.C. 1362 (destruction of communication lines, stations, or systems)

18 U.S.C. 1363 (injury to buildings or property within special maritime and territorial jurisdiction of the United States)

18 U.S.C. 1366(a) (destruction of energy facilities)

18 U.S.C. 1751(a),(b),(c), or (d) (Presidential and Presidential staff assassination, kidnaping, or assault)

18 U.S.C. 1992 (terrorist attacks on trains and mass transit)

18 U.S.C. 2155 (destruction of national defense materials, premises, or utilities), 2280 (violence against maritime navigation)

18 U.S.C. 2281 (violence against maritime fixed platforms)

18 U.S.C. 2332 (certain homicides and other violence against United States nationals occurring outside of the United States)

18 U.S.C. 2332a (use of weapons of mass destruction)

18 U.S.C. 2332b (acts of terrorism transcending national boundaries)

18 U.S.C. 2339A (providing material support to terrorists)

18 U.S.C. 2339B (providing material support to terrorist organizations)

18 U.S.C. 2340A (torture committed under color of law)

42 U.S.C. 2284 (sabotage of nuclear facilities or fuel)

49 U.S.C. 46502 (aircraft piracy)

49 U.S.C. 46504 (second sentence)(assault on a flight crew with a dangerous weapon)

49 U.S.C. 46505 (explosive or incendiary devices, or endangerment of human life by means of weapons, or aircraft)

49 U.S.C. 46506 (certain criminal laws to acts on aircraft)

49 U.S.C. 60123(b) (destruction of interstate gas or hazardous liquid pipeline facility)

2. *Federal Crimes of Terrorism That Do Not Result in or Involve the Risk of Death or Serious Injury*

18 U.S.C. 32 (destruction of aircraft or aircraft facilities)

18 U.S.C. 37 (violence at international airports)

18 U.S.C. 81 (arson within special maritime and territorial jurisdiction)

18 U.S.C. 175 or 175b (biological weapons offenses)

18 U.S.C. 175c (variola virus)

18 U.S.C. 229 (chemical weapons offenses)

18 U.S.C. 351(a),(b),(c), or (d) (congressional, cabinet, and Supreme Court assassination and kidnaping)

18 U.S.C. 831 (nuclear materials offenses)

18 U.S.C. 832 (participation in a foreign atomic weapons program)

18 U.S.C. 842(m) or (n) (plastic explosives offenses)

18 U.S.C. 844(f)(2) or (3) (arson and bombing of federal property)

18 U.S.C. 844(i) (burning or bombing of property used in, or used in activities affecting, commerce)

18 U.S.C. 956(a)(1) (conspiracy to murder, kidnap, or maim persons abroad)

18 U.S.C. 1203 (hostage taking)

18 U.S.C. 1361 (destruction of federal property)

18 U.S.C. 1362 (destruction of communication lines, stations, or systems)

18 U.S.C. 1363 (injury to buildings or property within special maritime and territorial jurisdiction of the United States)

18 U.S.C. 1366(a) (destruction of energy facilities)

18 U.S.C. 1751(a),(b),(c), or (d) (Presidential and Presidential staff assassination and kidnaping)

18 U.S.C. 1992 (terrorist attacks on trains and mass transit)

18 U.S.C. 2155 (destruction of national defense materials, premises, or utilities),

18 U.S.C. 2156 (production of defective national defense material)

18 U.S.C. 2280 (violence against maritime navigation)

18 U.S.C. 2281 (violence against maritime fixed platforms)

18 U.S.C. 2332 (certain homicides and other violence against United States nationals occurring outside of the United States)

18 U.S.C. 2332a (use of weapons of mass destruction)

18 U.S.C. 2332b (acts of terrorism transcending national boundaries)

18 U.S.C. 2332f (bombing public places)

18 U.S.C. 2332g (anti-aircraft missiles)

18 U.S.C. 2332h (radiological dispersal devices)

18 U.S.C. 2339 (harboring terrorists)

18 U.S.C. 2339A (providing material support to terrorists)

18 U.S.C. 2339B (providing material support to terrorist organizations)

18 U.S.C. 2339C (financing terrorism)

18 U.S.C. 2339D (receipt of military training from a foreign terrorist organization)

18 U.S.C. 2340A (torture committed under color of law)

21 U.S.C. 960A (narcoterrorism)

42 U.S.C. 2122 (atomic weapons)

42 U.S.C. 2284 (sabotage of nuclear facilities or fuel)

49 U.S.C. 46502 (aircraft piracy)

49 U.S.C. 46504 (second sentence) (assault on a flight crew with a dangerous weapon)

49 U.S.C. 46505(b)(3) or (c) (explosive or incendiary devices, or endangerment of human life by means of weapons, or aircraft)

49 U.S.C. 46506 (if homicide or attempted homicide involved, application of certain criminal laws to acts on aircraft)

49 U.S.C. 60123(b) (destruction of interstate gas or hazardous liquid pipeline facility)

7 years

18 U.S.C. 247 (damage to religious property)

18 U.S.C. 249 (hate crime not resulting in death)

18 U.S.C. 1031 (major fraud against the United States)

6 years

15 U.S.C. 77x (Securities Act violations)

15 U.S.C. 77yyy (Trust Indenture Act violations)

15 U.S.C. 78ff(a) (Securities Exchange Act violations)

15 U.S.C. 80a-48 (Investment Company Act violations

15 U.S.C. 80b-17 (Investment Advisers Act violations)

18 U.S.C. 1348 (securities and commodities fraud)

26 U.S.C. 6531 (tax crimes)

5 years

All crimes not otherwise provided for

1 year

18 U.S.C. 402 (contempt of court)

Appendix B. State Felony Statutes of Limitation

State	Felonies (Generally)	Various Exceptions (Not Exhaustive)
ALABAMA	3 years (Ala. Code §15-3-1)	Any time: (a) capital offense; (b) felony involving: - arson; forgery; drug trafficking; death or serious injury; use, attempted use, or threat to use violence; or counterfeiting; or (c) sex offense w/ victim <16 (Ala. Code §15-3-5)
ALASKA	5 years (Alaska Stat.§12.10.010)	(a) Any time: murder; kidnaping; class A, B, or unclassified felony sexual assault; felony sexual abuse of minor; various sexual offenses w/ a minor victim; (b) 10 years: 1st degree indecent exposure; manslaughter (Alaska Stat. §12.10.010)
ARIZONA	7 years (Ariz. Rev. Stat. Ann. §13-107)	Any time: attempted commission or commission of - homicide; class 2 felony sex offense or sexual exploitation of children; violent sexual assault; misuse of public money; felony falsification of public records (Ariz. Rev. Stat. Ann. §13-107)
ARKANSAS	(a) 6 years: Class Y or A crimes; (b) 3 years: Class B, C, D, or unclassified crimes (Ark. Code Ann. §5-1-109)	Any time: murder (Ark. Code Ann. §5-1-109)
CALIFORNIA	3 years (Cal. Penal Code §801)	(a) Any time: crime punishable by death or life imprisonment; or embezzlement of public money (b) 6 years: felony punishable by imprisonment for 8 years or more (Cal. Penal Code §§799, 800)
COLORADO	3 years (Colo. Rev. Stat. Ann. §16-5-401)	Any time: committing, attempting, conspiring to commit, or soliciting commit - murder, treason, kidnaping, forgery, or sex offenses against a child (Colo. Rev. Stat. Ann. §16-5-401)
CONNECTICUT	5 years (Conn. Gen. Stat. Ann. §54-193)	Any time: capital or class A felony; arson-murder; or 1st degree escape (Conn. Gen. Stat. Ann. §54-193)
DELAWARE	5 years (Del. Code Ann. tit. 11 §205)	Any time: commit or attempt to commit murder, class A felony, or a sexual offense (Del. Code Ann. tit. 11 §205)

State	Felonies (Generally)	Various Exceptions (Not Exhaustive)
FLORIDA	3 years (Fla. Stat. Ann. §775.15)	(a) Any time: capital or life felony, felony resulting in death, or perjury in a capital case;
		(b) 10 years: felony from use of destructive device resulting in injury;
		(c) 4 years: 1st degree felony, (Fla. Stat. Ann. §775.15)
GEORGIA	4 years (Ga. Code Ann. §17-3-1)	(a) Any time: murder;
		(b) 15 years: rape;
		(c) 7 years: other crimes punishable by death or life imprisonment; or felonies w/ victims <14 (Ga. Code Ann. §17-3-1)
HAWAII	3 years (Haw. Rev. Stat. §701-108)	(a) Any time: commit, attempt, conspire to commit, or solicit murder;
		(b) 10 years: vehicular manslaughter;
		(c) 6 years: class A felony (Haw. Rev. Stat. §701-108)
IDAHO	5 years (Idaho Code §19-402)	Any time: murder, voluntary manslaughter, rape, sexual abuse of a child, or terrorism (Idaho Code §19-401)
ILLINOIS	3 years (Ill. Comp. Stat. Ann. ch. 720 §5/3-5)	Any time: homicide, attempted murder, treason, arson, or forgery (Ill. Comp. Stat. Ann. ch.720 §5/3-5)
INDIANA	5 years (Ind. Code Ann. §35-41-4-2)	Any time: murder or a Class A felony (Ind. Code Ann. §35-41-4-2)
IOWA	3 years (Iowa Code Ann. §802.3)	(a) Any time: murder;
		(b) 10 years: sexual abuse (Iowa Code Ann. §§802.1, 802.2, 802.3)
KANSAS	5 years (Kan. Stat. Ann. §21-5107)	Any time: murder, terrorism, use of weapons of mass destruction (Kan. Stat. Ann. §21-5107)
KENTUCKY	Any time (Ky. Rev. Stat. Ann. §500.050)	
LOUISIANA	4 years (La. Code Crim. P. art. 572)	(a) Any time: crime punishable by death or life imprisonment;
		(b) 30 years: various sex crimes against minors;
		(c) 6 years: felony punishable at hard labor) (La. Code Crim. P. arts. 571, 571.1. 572.)

State	Felonies (Generally)	Various Exceptions (Not Exhaustive)
MAINE	(a) 6 years: Class A, B, or C crime; (b) 3 years: Class C or D crime (Me. Rev. Stat. Ann. tit. 17-A §8)	Any time: murder, 1st or 2d degree homicide, or various sexual offenses against a minor (Me. Rev. Stat. Ann. tit. 17-A §8)
MARYLAND	Any time subject to occasional individual statutory exceptions, e.g., computer crimes (3 years) (Md.Cts. & Jud. Proc. §5-601)	
MASSACHUSETTS	6 years (Mass. Gen. Laws Ann. ch. 277 §63)	(a) Any time: murder (b) 15 years: commit or conspire to commit rape or assault w/ intent to rape or murder; (c) 10 years: commit or conspire to commit robbery or assault w/ intent to rob (Mass. Gen. Laws Ann. ch. 277 §63)
MICHIGAN	6 years (Mich. Comp. Laws Ann. §767.24)	(a) Any time: murder, terrorism, or 1st degree sexual conduct; (b) 10 years: kidnaping, extortion, conspiracy or assault w/ intent to murder (Mich. Comp. Laws Ann. §767.24)
MINNESOTA	3 years (Minn. Stat. Ann. §628.26)	Any time: crime resulting in death, kidnaping (Minn. Stat. Ann. §628.26)
MISSISSIPPI	2 years (Miss. Code Ann. §99-1-5)	Any time: murder, rape, kidnaping, arson, manslaughter, burglary, aggravated assault, forgery, counterfeiting, robbery, larceny, fraud, embezzlement, or various sexual offenses against minors (Miss. Code Ann. §99-1-5)
MISSOURI	3 years (Mo. Ann. Stat. §556.036)	Any time: murder, rape or a class A felony (Mo. Ann. Stat. §556.036)
MONTANA	5 years (Mont. Code Ann. §45-1-205)	(a) Any time: homicide (b) 10 years: sexual assault (Mont. Code Ann. §45-1-205)
NEBRASKA	3 years (Neb. Rev. Stat. §29-110)	Any time: treason, murder, arson, forgery or various sexual offenses (Neb. Rev. Stat. §29-110)
NEVADA	3 years (Nev. Rev. Stat. Ann. §171.085)	(a) Any time: murder, terrorism, rape; (b) 5 years: kidnaping, attempted murder; (c) 4 years: theft, arson, robbery, burglary, sexual assault, or forgery (Nev. Rev. Stat. Ann. §§171.080, 171.085)

State	Felonies (Generally)	Various Exceptions (Not Exhaustive)
NEW HAMPSHIRE	6 years (N.H. Rev. Stat. Ann. §625:8)	Any time: murder (N.H. Rev. Stat. Ann. §625:8)
NEW JERSEY	5 years (N.J. Stat. Ann. §2C:1-6)	(a) Any time: murder, manslaughter, sexual assault
		(b) 10 years: environment offenses; (c) 7 years: bribery or certain other offenses involving misconduct in office (N.J. Stat. Ann. §2C:1-6)
NEW MEXICO	(a) 6 years: 2d degree felony; (b) 5 years: 3d or 4th degree felony (N.M. Stat. Ann. §30-1-8)	Any time: capital or 1st degree felony (N.M. Stat. Ann. §30-1-8)
NEW YORK	5 years (N.Y. Crim. P. Law §30.10)	Any time: class A felony or 1st degree rape, sexual criminal act, or sexual conduct against a child (N.Y. Crim. P. Law §30.10)
NORTH CAROLINA	Any time (no statute)	
NORTH DAKOTA	3 years (N.D. Cent. Code §29-04-02)	Any time: murder (N.D. Cent. Code §29-04-01)
OHIO	6 years (Ohio Rev. Code Ann. §2901.13)	(a) Any time: murder;
		(b) 20 years: commit, attempt, or aid and abet kidnaping, robbery, riot, manslaughter, sexual assault, burglary, or arson (Ohio Rev. Code Ann. §2901.13)
OKLAHOMA	3 years (Okla. Stat. Ann. tit. 22 §152)	(a) Any time: murder;
		(b) 12 years: rape, sodomy, or certain other sexual offenses (Okla. Stat. Ann. tit. 22 §§151, 152)
OREGON	3 years (Ore. Rev. Stat. §131.125)	(a) Any time: commit, attempt, conspire to commit, or solicit murder;
		(b) variable: various sexual offenses against minors;
		(c) 6 years: arson (Ore. Rev. Stat. §131.125)
PENNSYLVANIA	2 years (Pa. Stat. Ann. tit. 42 §5552)	(a) Any time: commit, conspire to commit, or solicit murder; manslaughter; or aggravate assault of a police officer;
		(b) 12 years: major sex offenses;
		(c) 5 years: major offenses (Pa. Stat. Ann. tit. 42 §§5551, 5552)

State	Felonies (Generally)	Various Exceptions (Not Exhaustive)
RHODE ISLAND	3 years (R.I. Gen. Laws §12-12-17)	(a) Any time: treason, homicide, arson, burglary, counterfeiting, forgery, robbery, rape, assault, drug trafficking, or any other felony punishable by life imprisonment; (b) 10 years: larceny, bribery, racketeering, perjury, or extortion (R.I. Gen. Laws §12-12-17)
SOUTH CAROLINA	Any time (no statute)	
SOUTH DAKOTA	7 years (S.D. Cod. Laws §23A-42-2)	Any time: Class A, B, or C felonies (S.D. Cod. Laws §23A-42-2)
TENNESSEE	(a) 15 years: Class A felony; (b) 8 years: Class B felony; (c) 4 years: Class C or D felony; (d) 2 years: Class E felony (Tenn. Code Ann. §40-2-101)	Any time: crime punishable by death or life imprisonment (Tenn. Code Ann. §40-2-101)
TEXAS	3 years (Tex. Code Crim. P. art. 12.01)	(a) Any time: murder, manslaughter, rape, certain human trafficking offenses, or various sexual offenses against minors; (b) 10 years: forgery, embezzlement, arson (Tex. Code Crim. P. art. 12.01)
UTAH	4 years (Utah Code Ann. §76-1-302)	Any time: capital felony, murder, manslaughter, or kidnaping (Utah Code Ann. §76-1-301)
VERMONT	3 years (Vt. Stat. Ann. tit.13 §4501)	(a) Any time: rape, murder, arson(causing death), or kidnaping; (b) 11 years: arson; (c) 6 years: certain sexual offenses, grand larceny, robbery, burglary, embezzlement, forgery, bribery, false claims, fraud, or felony tax offenses (Vt. Stat. Ann. tit.13 §4501)
VIRGINIA	Any time (Va. Code §19.2-8)	
WASHINGTON	3 years (Wash. Rev. Code Ann. §9A.04.080)	(a) Any time: homicide; (b) 10 years: arson, rape, or certain offenses involving misconduct in office; (c) until the victim is 28 years of age: certain sexual offenses against minors (Wash. Rev. Code Ann. §9A.04.080)
WEST VIRGINIA	Any time (no statute)	

State	Felonies (Generally)	Various Exceptions (Not Exhaustive)
WISCONSIN	6 years (Wis. Stat. Ann. §939.74)	(a) Any time: 1st degree murder, felony murder
		(b) various times: certain sex offenses committed against a child (Wis. Stat. Ann. §939.74)
WYOMING	Any time (no statute)	

Author Contact Information

Charles Doyle
Senior Specialist in American Public Law
cdoyle@crs.loc.gov, 7-6968

www.ingramcontent.com/pod-product-compliance
Lightning Source LLC
Chambersburg PA
CBHW081244180526
45171CB00005B/538